GCODE

RYAN STEWMAN

G Code

© 2020 Ryan Stewman

ISBN 9798607706265

Disclaimer

The advice and events outlined in this book are for informational purposes only. The reader relies on said advice and circumstances at his/her own risk. The results of taking any actions outlined in this book may vary and the author and publisher make no guarantees regarding any results.

Cover Concept: Sooraj Mathew

Cover Design: Cody Toussau

Preliminary Editor: Hilary Jastram

Final Editor: Lori Lynn

"There are only 7 colors and 10 numbers.
Life is simple.
It's humans that make it complicated."
— *Ryan Stewman*

CONTENTS

INTRODUCTION

Life is a code.

We live by a code.

Everything on this planet is a code.

Even our governing laws are codes, yet we never look for a code to live our lives by.

It's ironic.

Because living by a code is the key to getting what you want, when you want it.

That's why I knew you needed to read this book and why I wrote it. Within these pages, I am going to outline for you exactly how your life could be and what you could experience if you stick to a code. This is information that is critical to how you experience your life, and it is so simple to implement. There are actually only four parts to remember.

These parts have meaning and are easy to understand, and I'm going to spend some time really defining them for you, so you'll *completely* understand them, unlike the vague buzzwords flying around like "level up" or "10X."

Knowing exactly what we mean when we're talking about goals is paramount to reaching those goals.

When we're looking for success or trying to define it, we don't often have a clear focus on the exact meaning of terms and how we're supposed to apply them to our lives. It might not sound like a big deal, but it is. We can't get clear on what exactly it is that we want to be in life and how exactly we can live a fulfilled life without knowing what the hell we're talking about. Catchphrases won't get you any closer to learning who you are and what you're supposed to do.

My life has been filled with shit and curveballs. It's been filled with grief, loss, and heartbreak, but I have chosen not to focus on that anymore.

Even though for years, I *had* been focused on it.

We know that you get what you focus on, so you can guess what happened to me when the bad stuff was all I fixated on. I got more bad stuff. And when more bad stuff continued to happen, I continued to focus on more bad stuff. It was a horrible cycle that I couldn't escape from for decades of my life.

That pattern led to anxiety. Anxiety led to anger and feelings of desperation because I didn't know what the fuck I was going to do to escape the bullshit that I was putting myself through. Life was full of ups and downs, and I had no idea what to do to control them—until about three years ago. That's when my life was overrun with "ups." That's when I started understanding who I was meant to be, who I was called to be, and what I was supposed to do.

I had been distracted from this because all I was focused on was the stress that I kept inflicting on myself. I had been focused on how everything seemed to always go wrong and how there was too much going wrong in my life.

Then I broke the cycle through the discovery of the G Code.

Now that I'm living a new reality overflowing with good, it's my duty to pass this knowledge on to you.

The first fact that I want you to know is that distractions are killing you. This might seem really overwhelming to hear because life is full of distractions. But you can't give in to them—no matter how many there are—because when you do, those distractions take your power away.

The second fact that I want you to know is that your power is your ability to focus.

When you're not focused, you're not productive. And when you're not productive, you can't win.

It took me a long time to learn that, but the second I recognized that I could change and that I could use focus to create a huge advantage for myself, a really cool thing happened. My life got easier.

I didn't have to fight myself anymore, and that was great because I was sick of fighting. It was exhausting. Instead, I started looking for the right areas to focus on where I could excel —and eventually win. I defined every detail that mattered to me. I defined outcomes. I defined codes to live by. I defined the language that I would use. I defined thought patterns and drastically shifted my mindset. It took some doing, and I had to work to create a process that was effective. But I got there, and since then, I have changed the process even more in order to benefit you.

Now I'm bringing everything I've learned and everything I've tested on myself to you, through this book.

I know that whether you're holding this book in your hands in the form of a paperback, or reading my words in an e-book, or listening to my audiobook, this might just seem like some run-of-the-mill business book. I can assure you it's not.

This is not a regular book. It's for those who dare to be great. This book is almost like a religious doctrine. It was created for you so you can live by the code I now live and die by. If you want the code that will finally work for you, it's not enough to simply read this book. You need to engage with the content from beginning to end and actually do what I teach you to do.

Once you understand the G Code and put every ounce of your power into action, you will be faced with a choice.

You can either decide to live by the code I've taught you, or you can live the rest of your life knowing that you're in violation of a code that can change your life—a code that can bring you everything you have ever dreamed of.

I encourage you to get out of your own way as you flip through these pages.

You know, people who read books are smart. This is both an advantage and a disadvantage because the smarter you are, the harder it is to believe that life can be as simple as I'm telling you it is. The smarter you are, the more you will want to reject that this code can be as effective as you want it to be. It can be and will be effective for you, just as it is for me, as long as you follow through with what I'm advising you to do. This is the code I have lived by that has made my life what it is today. This is the code that I'm asked about by so many different people who want to know what I'm doing so they can experience the level of success that I now have. It's not luck. It's a code.

I'm bringing you this code because I know it will work for you. Part of the reason it will work so well for you is that it's uncomplicated. When I put this process together for you, I made sure it would be uncomplicated by using minimal pieces of the puzzle, easy-to-understand goals, and simple conditioning.

I've been blessed with one talent that's greater than any other talent I have—and that's taking complex processes and breaking them down to their simplest forms. This is exactly what I'm going to do for you in this book.

I'm going to break down how the world works.

I'm going to break down how your mind works.

I don't need a PhD. I don't need a doctorate in psychology. Neither do you.

I can tell you how the world works from real-world experience, meditation, soul-searching, therapy, books, seminars, mentors, models, and role models. What I'm about to share with you is going to snap right into place, just like a puzzle piece.

I'm going to open up how your mind works and help you dissect your thought patterns. When you put into practice what I'm about to share with you, it will turn you into a completely different person—a person who is the best version of you.

If you simply stick to the code for one year after reading this book, you'll look back, and when you do, you won't see the same person looking back at you in the mirror.

You will not look the same.

You will not think the same.

You will not be the same.

You will not have the same desires.

You will feel fulfillment if, and only if, you live by the code in this book.

That's why I stress that you not only read this book to learn about the G Code—you need to live it and work it.

I already know what's going to happen to many readers of this book. It's the same thing that happens when any new product or service is rolled out. A lot of people are going to read the *G Code* and get all pumped up to implement what I'm teaching. But the changes aren't going to happen immediately for them; they'll get frustrated at not receiving instant gratification, and they'll violate the code and go back to their old patterns.

But the code is just like any computer program—if you violate it, the computer crashes.

I believe we're living in a simulation here on Earth, and we have to live by the G Code to not only stay operational but also to become the most elite versions of ourselves.

When you violate the code, your finances, relationships, health, and businesses crash. Your mindset gets corrupted, and your life is filled with hardships that seem like they follow you for years. You might feel like a victim of your own circumstances.

I don't want that for you. I know that's not why you're reading this book, just to return to average after giving it a shot. You don't want to settle back into your own little comfort zone. This book is going to challenge you to step out of that zone. It's going to give you actionable advice and a routine that you will live by every single day. But it will only help you if you take the action you're supposed to take.

The G Code does not discriminate. It doesn't care what color your skin is. It doesn't care what country you come from. It doesn't care how many genders you have. The G Code is here to do one job only—to give you the right areas of life to focus on. When you focus on the right things, as you will learn when you follow the code, you get to truly live a life of greatness.

I'm about to indoctrinate you with knowledge that's almost unbelievable and that will rely on bigger thinking than you've ever experienced before.

At the end of this book is a whole new world filled with everything that you've ever wanted: happiness, love, income, security, significance, and ultimately, your legacy.

But it's up to you to take action.

I'm going to talk a lot about focus in this book. When I do, I want you to know that focus isn't just channeled through your eyes. Focus means that you are taking action.

Focus means doing whatever it takes to make your vision manifest as a reality.

This book is going to change your life.

This book is going to spark a movement.

This book is going to rewire millions upon millions upon millions of minds.

It all starts with you, leading by example.

That's why you've got to take action on the G Code—you are a crucial part of the movement.

Give me one year of your life and the minimal investment of this book, and I'll show you a different person. This is the person that you can become just by living by a simple code. As unreal as it sounds, it's true.

I'm relying on you to lead this movement. Other people are relying on you, too. Lead by example. Show people that, if you can change, they can change. Let's all ascend into being the most elite versions of ourselves.

If you're going to let people know you are using the G Code by sharing the G Code hashtag, then you have to truly live it. We're not here to fake it until we make it. We're here to win. We're here to stick to the code and reap the benefits and the rewards that come as a result of committing to it.

I ask that you keep reading only if you're willing to live by the code, because once I explain it to you, there's no going back.

This isn't a book that's going to make you feel great about who you have been, although it will make you feel great. This isn't a book that's just about motivation, although it will motivate you. This isn't a book that's just about inspiration, although it will inspire you.

The premise of this book is greatness. We're born great. We're born with the ability to leave a lasting impression, to do notable things, and to possess a grateful mindset.

The G Code is the code to unlocking the greatness within us.

As my pastor friend, Keith Craft, always says, "The biggest robber of great is good." So many of us live in our comfort zone in familiar territory. We're used to the way things are. But as you'll learn, when you decide to become great, forces form against you. The force of average will try to hold you down, hold you back, control you, distract you, and sabotage your mission of greatness. But you can combat this force with the principles of this book that have been designed to last forever—far past the time this author is long gone and has lived his time on this planet.

This book is timeless. It can be opened at any time by anyone. It shows human beings how to live an elite way of life by opening it up, believing that it's true, and doing something about it. But it *starts* with a decision to be great.

You can have everything you want in life—from love to respect to power to money—but after you read this book, you'll also understand what is required in order to have those things. This isn't a secret manifestation book. This isn't a shortcut to everything that you want in life. These are the step-by-step daily principles that you must abide by if you want greatness out of this life.

I predict that you won't just read the G Code once. It needs to be read once a year and given as a gift to the people you love. This is a book that changes lives. It's that influential. And now you have the opportunity to change your life because it's in your hands. I'm excited that you're here. I'm excited that you've decided to give your attention to a book that can change your life and take your entire existence from good to great.

Greatness is within us all. It's within you, my friend, and as you turn the pages of this book and read the messages I have written just for you, you, too, will realize this greatness has been within you all along.

Now it's time for you to take your power back and show the world just how great you are. It's time for you to be prepared for what's about to happen in your life if you make the right decision and live by the G Code.

G CODE TESTIMONIALS

After a year of consistently living by the G CODE, I can attest that it has brought the completeness I was missing in my life! The G CODE is not a plan or challenge, but a way of life that can and will revolutionize the world!!!

—Brandon Gazaway

This shit has really opened my mind to a whole new level of thinking!

—Jason Norman

The G Code isn't just some feel-good list of things to do each day. It really is a way of life. The more you embrace it, the more you begin to embody it, and the more it 'magically' surrounds you.

—Marc Zalmanoff

————

Before I was introduced to this concept, I would get mentally hijacked by things outside of my control. It has literally transformed my life and made me unstoppable.

—Adam Niec

I'm only on day eight, but I have more focus, purpose, and momentum. Gratitude is such a key component.

—Brandon Bosworth

Been going through the G Code for about five months consistently. I'm in better shape. I have made significantly more money, my home life is better, and my level of focus is through the roof.

—Drewbie Wilson

Ryan gave me the blueprints to success, and it all started with the G Code. Every morning, as soon as I open my eyes, my thoughts immediately go to what I'm grateful for. My relationships have never been better. I'm in the best shape of my life, and my career is on a new level.

—Travis Hull

If you are looking to change your life, you need the G Code. If you're looking to level up, you need the G Code. If you're looking to have better relationships, better health, better sleep, better whatever, YOU NEED THE G CODE!

—Bryce Vance

1

CONDITIONING

When a baby elephant is tied to a stake in the ground, it's impossible for it to pull the stake up. That baby elephant will pull and tug, over and over again, but it will never be able to move that stake. And when this happens, its spirit breaks. The weird thing is that even when the elephant grows up into a giant that could easily pull up that same stake in the ground, it never attempts to. This is because, at a young age, the elephant learned it was impossible. Here's the kicker:

That elephant is you.

You learned at a young age that there was lots of stuff you couldn't do. You were trained to believe that a lot of what you hoped and dreamed of doing was impossible, so you came to believe it. That belief deepened in you over the years until one day, you stopped trying to push yourself to do anything bigger, to do anything that really meant anything to you, and that you most wanted to do. After that point, it never occurred to you to live your life any differently than the way you had been.

That's pretty depressing, isn't it?

That's exactly why I'm so thrilled that you're reading this book. You will soon have the tools to help yourself. Even better, as you keep reading, you'll learn how to end this kind of self-limiting mentality.

I'm going to unlock the doors for you and show you your possibilities. The fact that you're reading this book shows me that you're searching for these possibilities. You're wondering how you can live a more fulfilled life and, more importantly, escape the mentality of that baby elephant.

Speaking of stakes, what do the stakes in your life look like?

The stakes we're shackled to can take the form of many different messages and experiences. For example, when you were young, you may have been told:

"Money doesn't grow on trees."

"Money is the root of all evil."

Or, "It's easier for a camel to go through the eye of a needle than for a rich man to get into heaven."

In short, you were probably told that it takes a long time to make a lot of money. You probably saw that no matter how fast money came in, it went out even faster.

Everything you learned was bred into you at a young age by your parents, peers, teachers, and surroundings.

So what's the big deal? Why does it matter that you were told these things when you were a kid? You still had your whole life ahead of you, right?

If you learned that "money is not the key to happiness" but don't believe that's really true, you might have spent your whole life chasing money. You might think money *is* going to make you happy. But, once you had money in your hand, you learned the opposite. You learned that you've been wrong the whole time. Despite your fat wallet, you weren't happy. You weren't truly fulfilled. This is a negative event that stayed with you, and it influenced your mindset. After such disappointment, you stopped pursuing money because your frame of reference is that it won't make you feel fulfilled. This is an instance where you *thought you learned a truth.*

Now, here's the hell of it. You stop working for money, assuming it won't make a difference to the quality of your life, and so you suffer living on the fringe. But ... you learned the wrong truth.

Once we adopt a value like that, it's hard to change our minds again, and we can go through our lives living for the wrong thing and searching for what we *think* can make us happy. We overcomplicate what it takes to be happy.

Take heart as you read on, because I know that from your head to your heart to your toes, it is possible to be happy. Money is not the root of all evil. Lack of money is the root of all evil. Lack of love is the root of all evil. Most of us weren't loved correctly because the people who did love us just didn't know how to love us. Most of us don't even know how to regard money because we were spoon-fed lies.

Did you notice how I combined money, happiness, fulfillment, and love? That's because they're all interrelated.

This is one of the new truths that I want you to take in. This is one of the new truths embedded in these pages that will change your life.

I had the wrong idea about money, happiness, fulfillment, and love for way too many years of my life.

When I was five years old, my family had a lot of money. I got used to that as a little kid. My grandfather on my mother's side was a banker, and he owned several branches of banks. My other grandfather, on my father's side, was an entrepreneur, and he owned a glass factory. Our families were thriving. We owned ranches, horses, banks, buildings, properties, four-wheelers, swimming pools, forts, goats, dogs, cats, sheep, and fish. You name it, we had it.

Then, the crash of 1987 happened.

Savings and loans crashed all over the country. It was much like the financial debacle of 2008. Everything went to shit. My banker grandfather lost his banks. My other grandfather, who had loans tied to those banks, lost his business.

Our whole family fell apart. I watched them get hit hard while I was still young and impressionable—like a baby elephant. In no time at all, my family went from thriving to barely surviving.

It didn't matter that my family was smart. Because of how hard everyone had been hit, options to recover were limited. My family was reduced to doing the best they could with what they had. My banker grandfather, who had been in the Navy, went back to college on the GI Bill. My other grandfather started another business and eventually became successful again.

I watched this all unfold and learned at a young age that everything you have can be taken away from you in an instant.

I also learned that when you lose everything, financial turmoil follows. My parents fought because of it. Then my father divorced my mother and split. I wouldn't see him again for 15 or 20 years. Later in my life, I learned that I had abandonment issues because of these circumstances.

At a young age, one of the stakes that held me back was abandonment. It froze me to the spot. I couldn't trust that life wouldn't change. I couldn't trust that I wouldn't lose people and everything else that mattered to me. In my mind, everything in my life had abandoned us. Money abandoned us. My own father abandoned us. We had to abandon the town that we lived in because my banker grandfather, who had lost his business, had lost a lot of other people's money, too. We had to abandon our closest relationships; I had to leave my school, abandon my friends, and even my cousins. All at once, I was abandoned in every possible area of life.

All of a sudden, it was weird celebrating Christmas. My dad wouldn't show up, but I still saw my grandparents. It got weirder still when my mother remarried and my stepdad adopted me. He didn't understand me. He didn't really know me. And he was abusive. That made my life really hard. He would tell me that he loved me and that I was his son, but I will never forget the day that he choked me until my eyes bled from the inside.

All these stakes that formed as a result of this financial crash metaphorically anchored me as the baby elephant. Abandonment, loss of security, and betrayal were the stakes that held me in place for years. They were the stakes that I thought I couldn't detach from—but they ultimately made me who I am today. I had to work harder than I ever had before in order to overpower their hold on me, and I did. But it was a struggle to get here.

I learned so many negative things when I was in that baby elephant phase between the ages of three and seven—exactly when we learn everything about life. It doesn't matter what happens in your life during that time, you will learn from it. And you will take what you've learned and turn it into a value. That means that until something dramatic happens in your life, be it divorce, a health scare, a penitentiary stint, facing court, or something else drastic in nature, you will never rewire the way of thinking that took root in you between those ages. Unless you are exposed to a new way of thinking through a disruptive event in your life, you will keep living with the same values you developed between the ages of three and seven. Even as you mature, you will not change, even though being such a young kid was so long ago.

My goal is to make the moment you picked up this book the moment your rewiring began. When you hold this book in your hands, I want you to feel the change that can improve and affect your life. When you feel this change, it will cause you to think bigger, and that will cause you to change your mindset. That's the point of this book; it's the catalyst you've been looking for. The information in the coming chapters will change the game. It will unlock the doors to your mind, just the way it unlocked the doors to mine.

The mind is great because it's like a combination lock.

I put combination locks on the front doors of each of my investment properties. These locks use 10 digits that can be combined in different ways in only four slots, but there are hundreds upon thousands of combinations that can be created from those 10 digits in those four slots. You have to use the right code to unlock the right door before you can open it.

Our minds operate in the same way. The words we hear are nearly always the same. We rarely pick up any new ones. We can only see a handful of colors with different shades and values within those colors.

If we see roughly 10 colors, and we use 10 digits, we know that we're exposed to these colors and digits over and over again. We don't see anything new. But what if one day we did see a new color or were told about a new number?

Maybe that would lead us to just the right combination to unlock some different possibilities and opportunities we can't even fathom.

Doesn't it make sense that the right combination of words might be the perfect combination that unlocks your way of thinking and even unlocks your true potential? The combination of the code of the usual elements—the words we hear and use— is where the magic lies.

The G Code is that code for you. It's the right combination of words that you need to hear to spark epiphanies and activate the catalyst for change in your life. This book will open the vault to the riches within you.

But before you can spin the combination on the lock and access the code, you must break free from the thinking that you learned at a young age that has shackled you ever since.

As you read this book, you're not only going to learn new stuff. You're also going to be forced to unlearn old stuff. What I share will challenge you. And as you'll soon learn when I introduce you to a concept that I call the force of average, that force is going to make it difficult to stay focused on what you are learning. One of the laws of the force of average is that the bigger the mission, the bigger the distraction. And this is why as you take in more information about the G Code, you'll find it more difficult to pay attention.

You probably still think like a seven-year-old, but you don't realize it because you're in a body that's fully matured. While your body has changed, your mind hasn't changed the way it has processed thoughts since you were seven. Let me help you with this. Let me hand you the tool that will change your life.

So many books have been published that claim to contain new information designed to help you improve your life that you likely experience a level of disbelief and skepticism when you hear about them. This is the same effect that takes place when you see a guy in a Ferrari driving down the road. The first thought in your mind might be, *What a douchebag.* When you see that Ferrari, you immediately become skeptical about the kind of person he is. That's a certain kind of wiring that's impacting your thoughts. It's this kind of thinking that we all get sucked into from time to time that proves why your mind needs to be rewired. Somewhere along the way, you made the association between Ferrari and douchebag, just the same way that you make other associations based on what happened when you were young. What's really shocking about what I've just shared with you is that the people who programmed your mind—all the adults who influenced you —are nowhere near the level that you're on right now. It's time to change what you allow to influence you. It's time to let go of childhood beliefs that haven't served you in decades.

As you unlearn the information you were programmed with, you will replace it with new information. The goal is not to start with a clean slate, erasing everything you've learned. Instead, we'll take out what you don't need and what's holding you back, and we'll put in something better.

Think of it this way, we're going to remove an 8-cylinder engine from a vehicle and put in a 12-cylinder turbocharged engine instead. After all, the mind is a machine, just like a car. Once you bend the barriers, escape what you learned in the wonder years, and rewire your thinking for modern times and the future, the game completely changes for you. Windows open up. The combination of words that unlocks your mind also unlocks unlimited possibilities in your life so you can unleash your true potential.

This book will establish that we're going to live by a code— not the code that was ingrained in you when you were young, not the code that your parents, peers, teachers, or anybody else that you respected when you were growing up taught you. No, this is a code that exists for a reason. This is a code that cannot be hacked or cracked. This code has to be abided by. That's the difference between the information you have in your hands right now and every other book on the shelf.

You're not a baby elephant anymore. You can pull up that stake. You can move mountains. If a piece of grass can break through concrete because it's genetically coded to seek water and light, then you can bust through any barrier—no matter how big or strong it is. Your mind is fortified to do whatever you deem possible. As long as you stay focused, you will experience a predictable outcome.

It's time to break free from that stake that's been holding you back since you were a baby elephant. It's time to emerge into the giant beast you were born to be.

2

THE FORCE OF AVERAGE

The G *Code* is more than a book. It's more than a manual for your life; it's more like the Bible. You need it to show you what you need to do in your life in order to enjoy your life to the fullest. If you religiously follow what I teach you in this book, your perspective will shift, and you will go on to become the best and most elite version of yourself.

If you are a religious person, that's awesome. I work with people who hold all types of beliefs, and I respect them all—as long as they are not harmful to anyone else. All I ask is that as I share the inner workings of the G Code with you, you open your eyes to a different way of thinking besides traditional religious beliefs. This thinking might go against what you believe, or it might align with what you believe. Regardless, please take off your religious lenses as you read or listen to this book.

You will see very shortly that I break down the complicated universal workings of the world so simply that even the youngest eyes and ears will completely understand and grasp my message. We don't need a 2000-page book that nobody understands telling us how life works on this planet.

As I stated before, smart people tend to discredit simpler concepts because they believe *it can't be that easy*. That's why I don't want you to read this book from a religious or skeptical perspective. When you read the *G Code*, it's imperative that you do so with an open mind to gain an understanding of what you are consuming.

It might feel a little awkward, but you need to have blind faith that what I'm about to teach you might actually be true. Then, when you're done reading, if you have enough faith to actually take the steps to do what I'm about to teach you, your life could become fulfilling and happy. You could even have everything you want on this planet. Because you cracked open this book, I know that you want to make a change; now, what if I told you that I'm about to teach you everything you need to know to overhaul your life, but being skeptical will hold you back? That's how critical it is that you take in this content with a mind that is wide open.

Now that your mind is open, we can get started because you are closer to where you need to be.

First, let's assume that this planet we're living on—Earth—is a microchip inside a server. I know it sounds out there, but hear me out and keep your receptive mindset going.

My friend, Howard Getson, is insanely intelligent and a bit of an anomaly. He has PhD's in engineering and coding artificial intelligence and runs Capitalogix, an artificial intelligence hedge fund out in Coppell, Texas. His company buys and sells stocks within nanoseconds at a million times the pace you and I could buy them through a company like Charles Schwab or E-Trade. Howard only works with the most elite of millionaires.

His office doesn't have a trading desk or a sales floor, but that's just one example of how he operates differently. If you walk around to the back of his office, you'll find the reason why his internet is a million times faster than the internet you use.

He's plugged directly into the servers. If you head back to where all his servers are, you'll see they're all black machines. These servers look like huge filing cabinets with blue blinking lights. Each one of those blue blinking lights represents artificial intelligence inside a microchip.

When I learned this, I thought, *What if we're all just artificial intelligence inside a microchip?* It makes sense if you think about it.

Before you scoff at me, take a moment one of these nights, and look out the window into outer space. Check out all the stars. They look just like those blue and white lights shining throughout Howard's server office.

So, let's assume that we're a part of a simulation for a minute, meaning that the world we live in is controlled and part of a bigger universe. In a sense, this would mean that we're not real. I don't mean that we don't have genuine feelings. We are tangible people on Earth and in life. I mean that anytime you code artificial intelligence or a simulation, creation is happening. Whether you believe God, Allah, or a different entity created Earth, we came to be. To paraphrase Tony Robbins, if you think that there is no God and something didn't create us, that's like thinking the dictionary came to be because a tornado went through a paper factory.

We know something created us, but what if we were created at the hands of a master coder, someone like Mark Zuckerberg or Bill Gates? What if we are alive in our own simulation?

For the purpose of what I'm going to teach you in this book, let's just pretend that in 2020, this is the reality over any reality we might perceive or any other reality that's been presented to us.

It follows then that any time you're going to create a simulation, or an operation run on artificial intelligence, there will be set rules inside that coding. This concept is no different than when you play a video game.

We can all relate to getting to a certain point of a video game where you discover you're out of bounds and can no longer go on. This setup is similar to the commands and codes embedded within computer programs that predetermine the way a website looks and performs.

The same thing happens on this planet. An algorithm determines what our life is like and if we will reach the goals we set for ourselves, much like the Google algorithm that decides what search results are going to be shown on the first page. It's much like the Facebook algorithm, which shows you your favorite friends first. The algorithm on this planet is the Force oif Average, and the GCode is the way to beat it.

Before I go deep on you and explain every element that makes up this code, you need to understand that there's also opposition to this code—that opposition is called the force of average.

Imagine that this blue planet is perfectly coded and created so that everything is absolutely awesome all the time; we're living the lives we want to, and we're fulfilled in all the areas of life that matter the most to us. This is what would happen if we all followed the G Code and didn't deviate from what we were supposed to do because of the force of average. Each human being on this planet was coded and created to carry out a mission. To do this, the G Code must be followed and the opposition must be defeated every single day.

The force of average came to be when it was released on this planet as a virus. Since the beginning of time, that virus has infected the minds of human beings. It has infected the way we think. It has infected the way we do things. It has infected our confidence. It has infected our ability to receive love and to give love. This force of average has one job—just as all computer viruses do. Its only job is to show up and find one weakness, one breach in our security that keeps us focused and on track, and use it against us so that we fail in what we are assigned to do. It does this over and over and over again. The force of average has discovered the algorithm on this planet and knows how to destroy by repeatedly distracting us.

As human beings, we're born with one of the greatest, most powerful tools known to man. It's within each and every one of us, yet many of us spend our whole lives avoiding or not using this gift. The most powerful trait the creator has given us is focus. When you're a human being and can get in the zone and stay focused, you become unstoppable.

When Elon Musk got focused, he created cars that operate using the energy of the sun. His charging stations collect solar energy and convert it to electricity, which powers the electric cars so they can run. But how was Elon able to achieve this?

He was focused.

When Steve Jobs focused on changing the way smartphones operated, he got rid of flip phones. We now have iPhones, iPads, iMacs, and touchscreen everything because of Steve Jobs.

When Bill Gates said he was going to make everybody's life easier and create a user-friendly computer program that everybody across every channel could understand and use, he got focused and made it a reality.

When Jeff Bezos said he was going to create an online store that sold every conceivable product, it seemed crazy at the time. Nobody wanted to invest in it. Now he runs the biggest business in the world—all because he maintained his focus.

The force of average knows that when a human being is focused and in the zone, they're unstoppable. Its job is to stop human beings from progressing by using the temptation of distraction.

Think for a minute about the distractions you encounter in your life. You probably don't realize how distracted you are. You don't realize the subconscious programming that the force of average has instilled in you to keep you from being able to focus.

See if you can relate to these examples:

Ask yourself how many times in your life you've said, "I don't pay attention to the details; I'm the boss." You might feel that way (as though other people are paid to manage the details), but I'm telling you, it doesn't matter if you're the boss. You've got to focus on the details too, or things will get out of control.

Or maybe this sounds like you: "I'm having an ADD moment. I can't remember anything with my goldfish brain."

These are the messages you're constantly giving yourself because the force of average has infected you. It has reassured you that it's okay to use excuses to make yourself feel better about being off your game. Anytime you're not focused, you're distracted. And when you're distracted, you're not dedicated to fulfilling your mission. When you're not dedicated to fulfilling your mission, you can't carry out what you intended to do.

We need to know what's pulling at our attention before we can fix it, so let's talk about the areas where we get distracted.

"Digital Marketing experts estimate that most Americans are exposed to around 4,000 to 10,000 advertisements each day."[1] Addictions surround and distract us. Alcoholism, drugs, sex, and social media are all distractions. If you're focused on these things, you're not focused on what you were pre-programmed to do here on Earth. We'll go more in-depth about pre-programming in later chapters of this book, and then you'll discover what you're supposed to do on this planet. For now, let's dive back into the force of average because I need you to understand your true enemy.

A lot of people say the enemy is within. They don't mean that the enemy is you; they mean that we give in to urges that distract us. I agree with this statement. The force of average is within you. You're infected by it, and it's doing everything in its power to distract you at all times.

You'll want to keep reading because, in later chapters, I will also give you some tips to help you stay focused. It's imperative that you learn to focus; I can tell you from personal experience that when I stay focused, I can make whatever I want happen. I want you to be able to do the same, and I know that you can do the same. The only difference between you and me right now is my ability to focus. As you continue on in this book, you'll learn how to focus, too. Then you can talk about what you can accomplish when you're focused.

Beyond channeling the skill to focus, it's also important that you focus on the right things. So many people focus on the wrong things—things that don't serve them and even tear them down. They focus on the negative. They focus on the shit that keeps happening to them. They focus on being a victim. When they remain fixated on these things, they continue getting more and more shit dumped on them. Of course, this convinces them more than ever that they really are a victim. They are creating their existence because, as we are learning, whatever a human being focuses on, they get. The force of average distracts you from focusing on greatness; it tempts you to focus on bullshit. Cave into it, and that's exactly what you'll get. Bullshit.

But you weren't programmed to think this way about yourself. You know you haven't been this way your whole life. You've been infected.

I'm going to share with you how to heal that infection and how to rewire your mind so that you will no longer fall victim to the force of average.

This is not going to be easy, my friend. It's going to take a lot of dedication. It's going to take a lot of hard work. More importantly, it's going to take conjuring up your focus. But once I teach you what to focus on, you'll see that you have a choice. You can start your mission and live the best version of yourself and truly be elite, or you can give in to the force of average and forget about making your life better.

As I mentioned earlier, if you're in America, the force of average throws 4,000 to 10,000 advertisements your way every day. We also talked about how the force of average tempts you with addictions.

But we haven't included the distractions you fight off or the fact that the force of average is an early riser. First thing in the morning, when you wake up, you encounter challenges. If you have kids, they have problems right away—sometimes before your feet even hit the floor. The problems that they bring you to solve are an attempt to distract you from what you need to do. You end up juggling their issues and trying to get them to do what they need to do so you can maintain your schedule. They don't get dressed on time; they don't eat their breakfast. And of course, they're running late for school. Well, guess who has to drive them now? Guess who has even more time and attention taken away from what *they* are supposed to be doing? You! As the parent, you have to stop and find the time to fix what they screwed up. They're kids. Shit like this is going to happen, and you even expect it to happen, but it still pulls you away from where your focus needs to be. After all that, the morning's finally out of the way. The day goes on, but we're distracted almost 10,000 more times. You can see that it makes sense that we would be distracted so easily.

Unfortunately for us, the force of average is no fool. It understands that we have something called a Reticular Activating System (RAS). The RAS is the decision-making mechanism located inside your brain. Because of this mechanism, your brain is only good for a few thousand decisions every single day. Then it gets fatigued, just like any other muscle in your body.

If you don't think you make a few thousand decisions each

day, you're wrong. I'm counting all the little decisions that you probably discount. You have to think about what to eat, what time to go to the bathroom, what to wear, what shoes to put on, how you're going to log into the computer, what your password is, what you're going to write, what you're going to do, etc. This comprises thousands upon thousands of decisions that you're responsible for. These might not feel like decisions; they might feel more like automated actions you take. But if it requires your brain's engagement, it's a decision that can wear on your RAS.

All of these distractions lead to your RAS being weak and fatigued—this predisposes you to making bad decisions and focusing on the wrong stuff. This is a spiral that billions of people on this planet are falling victim to right now. In the past, the only answer was to go to a religious temple or *try* to understand a religious book. While I'm not anti-religion, I *am* pro-simplicity. I can't think of one religious book that's easy to understand, quick, to the point, and actionable. They don't exist because religious books have been intercepted by the force of average. Maybe the intention of the authors was to explain the inner workings of the universe. But the force of average infected them, and their teachings went all over the place and got complicated. It's impossible for the average Joe to understand them.

The G Code isn't simply a code. It's a movement. And when you learn about it, you'll also learn about the simplicity of this planet and how you can master and dominate it. Then you can go on to inspire and influence millions—all without laboring over an ancient book that you find impossible to understand.

I don't want to skip ahead though. Before I explain any more about how the G Code works, you first have to understand how the force of average works. You have to understand that as a human being, your focus is the most powerful weapon you possess. Distraction costs you time, money, love, and heartache —and it takes years off your life.

The force of average is strong. It's taken many powerful people down. Presidents caught up in sex scandals, world leaders charged with theft and money laundering, politicians falling from grace, and businessmen having it all and then losing everything all have one thing in common—the fact that they caved to the force of average.

If you're confused about the force of average, let me break it down into simpler terms that you might better relate to.

Have you ever had a good month in sales followed by a bad month? Have you ever found the love of your life only to end up fucking someone less attractive and making a huge mistake because you got drunk one night? Did you have a kid and promise to be the best dad in the world only to end up fighting with the kid's other parent and abandoning them both? Were you ever clean from an addiction for months before relapsing and repeating the cycle—getting clean and relapsing over and over again—ultimately being unable to kick the habit? Have you ever worked out consistently for months and started feeling better and looking better only to stop going to the gym? How about, have you ever stuck to a diet and lost weight only to quit your diet and put all the weight back on? Somehow, while you were focused on losing weight and following your diet, the force of average took you off track. These are all modern-day examples of how the force of average attacks people. It hits you in many different areas of life as you try to achieve specific goals. It doesn't matter the size of the goal. The only thing that matters is that it is a goal that means something to you. As long as you have a clearly defined goal that you're moving toward, the force of average will come at you.

Isn't it amazing that whatever our minds focus on and our bodies take action toward will be accomplished? It might not happen overnight, but as long as you maintain your focus, your aims will be accomplished. The force of average knows this, so its job is to distract you. If you're working on your fitness, you might have this thought in your head: *You look good. There's no need to work out as much anymore.* The force of average even gets into your subconscious. We hear the thought without even realizing it.

To understand why the force of average is so powerful, you need to know a bit about how your mind works.

Think about your conscious mind, meaning what you're processing as you read this book right now and everything else you're aware of in your environment—where you're sitting, what you're feeling, smelling, etc. Your conscious mind is like random access memory on a computer, AKA RAM. RAM searches your hard drive for whatever you tell it to search for and then brings up that program, picture, or document. The faster the RAM, the faster it can search through the hard drive. Today, hard drives can hold terabytes of information, so RAM has to be fast as shit to search through all the content on the hard drive. Understandably, some of our computers are slow if we have a lot of stuff on them.

Our conscious mind is the RAM. Our subconscious mind is the hard drive. Every experience, detail, feeling, *everything* that's ever happened to you is stored in your subconscious mind. Every positive and negative word ever said, every experience, good or bad, is saved on that hard drive, just like a computer. That's why when people take drugs like LSD, psychedelic mushrooms, or ayahuasca, the firewall separating the RAM and the hard drive disappears and the RAM and hard drive melt together as one, and this is not a good thing.

There has to be a firewall between the subconscious mind and the conscious mind because the conscious mind cannot handle all the data from the subconscious mind. Still, everything you've ever seen or experienced is logged, and when the conscious mind searches the subconscious mind for the memory it's trying to recall, sometimes it can't find it. That's a ton of stuff to sort through. We can't bring every experience we've ever had into our conscious world.

It's important that you understand this relationship between the RAM and the hard drive in your head because the force of average has infected your subconscious mind—but your conscious mind often doesn't know this.

Right now you're awake. You're reading this book or listening to it, but you have to practice focusing with your conscious mind. Beneath the surface of your conscious mind is the subconscious. When you're learning new information, you can't be bombarded with the old if you want to make the new information stick. This is why you need to focus.

As you go through these pages, you need to stay conscious so you can take in and retain what I'm talking about.

We're going to cover a lot of content that you can use to rewire your mind to understand and achieve conscious process-ing, then you will be able to get and stay focused on the right goals and move toward them intelligently. At the same time, we're going to rewire your subconscious anxiety to overcome the force of average and achieve greater control over your mindset. In short, you need the ability to focus on the conscious and be in the moment and learn without the intrusion of your subcon-scious mind—which, besides being filled with all of your memo-ries, also has the potential to distract you with all sorts of thoughts. We have to learn to control the subconscious mind if we want to stay the course.

Throughout this book, we're going to talk about the force of average a lot. For those of you who are avid social media users, go ahead and start using the hashtag #forceofaverage in your posts.

When shit happens to you, get in the habit of referencing it in your posts and comments with #forceofaverage. Doing this helps to identify what you're up against in your head and how many times you come up against it. It's one little tool that you can use to help you stick to the G Code and beat the force of average at its own game. Since the force of average's job is to distract you, you're going to learn how to be the most focused human being on the planet and beat it at its own game.

What I'm going to teach you encompasses very simple steps that have been broken down, giving you the tools to build an unstoppable focus. When you do this, you can get everything that you've ever wanted in your life. It really is that simple.

3

LANGUAGE IS CRITICAL

B efore we can jump into the heart of the G Code, you need
to understand the language that I'm going to use to talk
about it. One of the problems with many religious books and,
hell, even textbooks, business, and personal development books
is that they don't explain what they're talking about.

They just jump into the gist of it, and you can't fully grasp
the meaning behind the words. You have no choice but to take in
what you're reading on a surface level.

Before reading the prior chapter, you wouldn't have thought
that you needed to get deeply educated on what you're about to
read. The force of average would have sent a default message to
you that would sound something like: *I don't have to pay close
attention to this book.* Now that you've read a little about the force
of average, you know that's not true. You *do* need to focus and
pay close attention if you want to change the course of your life.

Before we continue, you need to be aware of the specific
meaning and algorithm of the force of average. That's why I
want you to take a minute to refocus on what you're reading, so

you don't do what the force of average is trying to convince you to do—which is to return to the status of being just "fine."

Let me explain. And pay attention to how I'm going to use the word "fine."

One Christmas, when I was about 23 years old, I sat down with my grandfather who used to be a banker.

I had just gotten into the banking business, and my grandfather was warning me. "Ryan," he said, "a lot of the signs out there right now in the market are similar to what happened to me in the 80s. In the 80s, when the S&Ls crashed, my banks went under. Now, notice that things are acting a lot like the 80s. I wouldn't be surprised if, in the next few years, everything crashes, so make sure you cover your ass."

I listened intently because I remembered going through the crash when I was so young.

He finished by saying to me, "You should know that the market always returns to fine."

I asked, "What do you mean by that?"

That's when he looked me in the eye and said, "'Returns to fine' means there's always a baseline. It might go up for a little while. It might fall down for a little while. But it always returns to fine. It returns to where the market's doing fine. Sometimes, the loan business is just fine. Or it might be great, and then suck. But most of the time, it returns back to fine."

Now that I'm a lot older and a lot more experienced, I can see the connection between what my grandpa shared and how the force of average gets us. It convinces us to "return to fine."

In this chapter, I'm going to help you understand what "fine" means in your life and what "elite" means, so we can train you to stay focused on elite. Every time you slip and fall, which you will, because that's part of life, you'll know where the thin line is between "fine" and where you must go above and beyond to reach "elite."

I'm going to walk you through a powerful exercise. Read or listen to the instructions first, then pause for a minute before you finish the exercise. I don't want you to rush right through it because it's a life-changing experience when you do it the right way.

I've done this exercise in front of tens of thousands of people on stages all across the country. Every time I get off the stage, people say this exercise changes everything in their lives. When I spoke in St. Louis at Ed Mylett and Andy Frisella's event, Arete Syndicate Live, the entire audience did this exercise. When I got offstage, Ed told me, "That was awesome. I'm going to do that with my people."

This is your opportunity to make a massive shift in your mind. Don't just read the next few paragraphs. Take the steps immediately, and then pick this book back up and jump in where you left off.

Here we go.

First, stand up straight and tall with your shoulders back. "Shoulders back" signifies confidence. Lock your shoulders back, even if it makes your posture feel weird.

Next, look over your right shoulder. Note that you only need to look over your right shoulder, not your left. Don't stare at anything in particular. Simply look over your right shoulder and then close your eyes. Closing your eyes is such an important part of this exercise.

Now, imagine that you clearly see the image of the most elite version of yourself standing next to you. What does that version of yourself look like?

Let's start at the feet. What do they look like? The toes, the ankles, the calves. Are your calves cut? Do you have nice legs? Are they shaved and tan? Take notice of your thighs, midsection, and stomach. Do you have ripped abs? Can you imagine what it feels like to be the most elite version of yourself?

Can you see yourself with a 6- or 12-pack? Are there veins in your forearms? Are you completely hairless and smooth as a dolphin with perfect tattoos? Whatever you want, observe this most elite version of yourself. This elite version of you is whoever you want to be.

Now imagine how you would dress yourself from head to toe. Would you wear the finest linens if you were the most elite version of yourself? Designer clothes? Would you wear a T-shirt and jeans? Shorts and flip-flops? Envision the most elite version of yourself. Now that you've got this person dressed, you can see what the most elite version of yourself looks like. Maybe you look younger. Maybe your hair is different. Maybe you're tanner. Maybe you're dressed nicer. Maybe your watch is upgraded, and so on.

Envision some other characteristics of this person.

Keep your eyes closed.

Continue looking at this person. They're looking straight ahead. You're looking at them. They have no idea you're there. While you're seeing this person, think about the love they must feel from others. The most elite version of yourself must be loved on very high levels, or that person couldn't be the most elite version of you. You want for nothing as this person, and that includes love. Think about all the love that comes from being the best you that you can possibly be.

Think about the people who are around you. Are you among celebrities? If you're the most elite version of yourself, are you around influencers, athletes, philosophers, religious leaders, politicians? Whatever the most elite version of yourself is, picture it in your mind. You might hang out with kings and presidents. You get to choose what this part of your life looks like because, since you're the best you can possibly be, you should have the best.

Think about your finances and how smoothly your business

is running because you're the most elite version of yourself. Envision how big your bank account is—how many zeros are there before the decimal point? What does it feel like to have such financial freedom?

You're taking care of the group of people around you, so there must be a massive amount of love in your heart and in your life. This love, abundance, and fulfillment extends into every area of your life. You're firing on all cylinders. Your machine is running, and it's smooth as silk. You're also the most elite version of your business self. You can't just pick a few areas that you want to be elite—for one part of your life to be elite, all parts must be elite.

Move on to envisioning the most elite version of your family and friends, the most elite version of your genetics, and the most elite version of your mind.

Are you sharp? Are you mentally tough like David Goggins? His childhood was a nightmare, but he went from depressed and overweight to becoming an elite athlete, Navy SEAL, Army Ranger, *and* Air Force Tactical Air Controller, as well as the author of the book *Can't Hurt Me*. Are you an effective communicator like best-selling author and world-renowned speaker Ed Mylett? Or celebrity coach Tony Robbins?

How much confidence would the most elite version of yourself feel? What is it like to walk into a room? Would you light it up? Would people be automatically drawn to you? When you're the most elite version of yourself, you're powerful. This means that people are magnetically drawn to you.

Now for the next step of this exercise.

Take one step to your right and put your feet in the exact place where the footprints of the most elite version of yourself stood. Now, look straight ahead, open your eyes, and become that version of yourself. Feel what it's like to be the most elite version of yourself. Cherish this moment for a minute. Embrace what it feels like to step into that power, knowing that you can have it all. Because it's true—you can.

What you just saw and created in your mind was what you were programmed to do on this planet. Who you are now is a reflection of how many times you've been distracted by the force of average.

The crazy thing about being the most elite version of ourselves is that, in reality, it's a carrot at the end of the stick. This is because we're constantly chasing this version of ourselves. As we level up, we get more elite, so we have to strive harder to reach an even more elite state. For example, if you're at 15% body fat, why not aim for 14.5%? If you quit smoking cigarettes, that's cool. Why not quit drinking, too? That's what I mean by chasing this more elite version of yourself.

I'm not saying that you have to think this way, but if you want to be the most elite version of yourself, you and I both know that you're going to have to leave a lot of things behind. You're going to have to break a lot of habits.

As you prepare to level up to this version of yourself, the force of average will try to convince you that your regular habits are okay and that you don't have to give up who you are. That's a preposterous way to think about yourself, and doing so is a guarantee that you'll return to "fine."

We can agree that everything's "fine" right now. Even though your house may be on fire, it's still fine. Most people sit on their couch watching TV and tell themselves, *It'll take care of itself and eventually burn out.* This fire represents the things that are going wrong that you need to fix to survive, so if you let it blaze on, you're in trouble. Instead of putting the fire out, people reassure themselves: *I'm fine.* This has to stop. We have to establish the baseline of what "fine" is so that we never return to that motherfucker again.

I don't want you there.

You don't want you there.

You're damn sure not going to leave a legacy by living a life of "fine."

But before we can refuse "fine" in our lives, we have to define what it is. We have to know the language surrounding "fine." This second exercise does a great job of helping you understand what feels "fine" and what feels "uncomfortable."

To identify your version of "fine," think about your financial comfort zone. How much money are you comfortable having in your bank account? You might think, *I'm comfortable with $10,000 in my bank account.* Go ahead and write that number down.

Think about the people in your comfort zone and who you're comfortable with. I'm uncomfortable as fuck when I'm around Ed Mylett. I'm uncomfortable as hell around Kent Clothier. When I'm around such high-level guys, I know I'm out of my comfort zone, which is exactly why I go there—to make myself uncomfortable and grow. Next, write down the people who are in your comfort zone—your drinking buddies, your homies from work, your gal pals. Write it all down. Nobody will ever see this but you.

Think about your relationship and what you're comfortable with. You might write something like, *I'm comfortable going on one date a month with my wife.* Whatever it is for you, your answer is fine. The goal is to ask yourself what's comfortable for you. Maybe you're comfortable with a wife or husband. Maybe you're comfortable just having somebody who lives with you. Maybe you want a person to bang occasionally. There's no judgment here. In answering these questions, it's imperative that you know what you're comfortable with. Be honest with yourself and write it down.

Think about other people in your house—if you're comfortable with or without kids, whether you want custody or not. Write it down.

Think about your diet and how you take care of yourself. You might think, *I'm comfortable eating fried chicken every night.* Fuck, aren't we all? Andy Frisella talks about loving french fries. This is comfortable for him and many other people because fries are comfort food. It doesn't matter what you want to eat the most, just write it down. I'm comfortable living on hot dogs and chicken fingers. Maybe you feel comfortable living on pasta and pizza. Your choice doesn't matter. The foods you write down should be what you could easily eat for the rest of your life. Write it down.

When you write down what you're comfortable with, it establishes your comfort zones in all the areas of your life. Once you know what these zones are, you can get the fuck out of them immediately. Before you can leave a comfort zone, you have to define it—otherwise you might not know that you're in that zone, so you wouldn't work on finding out what it is, because a comfort zone is so comfortable that it would never occur to you to leave.

Your comfort zones are going to vary because people are comfortable having different experiences, dollar amounts, and businesses. Right now, for example, I'm comfortable working both for somebody else and working for myself. Whatever your work comfort zone is, write it down.

Once you know what your comfort zone is in these areas, you'll realize how the force of average wants to distract you by keeping you nice and comfy. It probably tried to pull your attention away from creating your comfort zone list. The force of average wants to keep you from defining what your comfort zone is, and it wants to lie to you about how you don't have to leave it. That's why you might find answering these questions difficult at first. Try not to overthink your answers or get defensive about them. You simply want to be honest with yourself. When you do that, you'll be gold.

You might have said, or heard other people say, "That's out of my comfort zone." But most of the time, we don't know what we're talking about because we don't know what the fuck our comfort zone is in the first place. We've likely never taken the time to define what we're comfortable with. After completing this exercise, you can now understand what your comfort zones are.

The good news about knowing your comfort zones is that once you can recognize them, you can immediately trigger yourself to leave them.

The G Code was invented to keep you focused. We're going to define what you've lived with your entire life, those comfort zones that have kept you chained to "fine." Once you become aware of that thin line between "fine" and "elite," you'll move from unaware to aware. You'll know exactly what to expect and how to measure what you are doing. You will do nothing but improve as long as you determine to push yourself out of your comfort zone.

Let's go deeper.

What else are you comfortable with? Snacking? Not working out? I'm comfortable working out two times a week or once a month. I'm comfortable going on vacation every six months or every two years. Whatever you think about snacking and vacation, write it down. What about some other areas of your life? For instance, I'm comfortable living in a 3,000 square foot, $200,000 home. I'm comfortable driving a Ford F150 or a Toyota 4Runner. Write down what kind of home you're comfortable living in and what you're comfortable driving.

What kind of business network are you comfortable with? What kind of boss are you comfortable with?

Keep defining key areas of your life.

I'm taking you into the thought process of what the most elite version of yourself looks like. You'll begin to see what needs to be done to make this version of you happen and what work you need to do consistently to get there.

We're drawing a line between your comfort zone and what's outside of it. This means whatever you're comfortable with is whatever you just wrote down. When you say, "I'm fine," that's the level that you feel comfort at. You might be comfortable with $5,000 in your bank account and making $50,000 a year. You might be comfortable with $100,000 in your bank account and making $250,000 a year. It doesn't matter because it's a fact that you'll sell your dream for a dollar amount so you can be "fine" and return to that comfort zone.

Since we've now defined your fine line, we've defined your comfort zone. For example, in terms of what you're comfortable with in your bank account, when you have less than that specified "fine" dollar amount in your bank account, you're out of your comfort zone and willing to work. But what happens when you have more than that dollar amount in your account? This is when people overspend to get back to that feeling of "fine" in their financial life.

If you want to change what your money comfort zone is, you need to change your comfort zone levels.

Here's an example:

When you level up, you have to change your comfort zone levels. If you were originally comfortable with $5,000 and then you make more than $5,000, you have to learn to get comfortable at $10,000. Once you accumulate $10,000 and get comfortable with it, you have to learn to get comfortable with $25,000.

The goal is to always stay uncomfortable.

Uncomfortable is your new baseline.

You cannot return to "fine." Anytime you slip and think, *Oh shit, I don't have people who love me. I'm in a miserable job, and I don't have enough money,* I want you to condition yourself to respond to that voice with: *This isn't my comfort zone. It's actually a fucking nightmare. This is what I'm used to, and I am not accepting that reality anymore.*

In reality, your comfort zone is not a comfort zone at all. It's a sedation tool used by the force of average to distract you from becoming the person that you saw standing to your right—so that you can say, "I'm fine."

Recently, a hip-hop artist named Nipsey Hussle passed away. He was a legend on the streets of Compton, a guy who started businesses in the area that birthed him. He helped people, gave back, and was a hero in the hood.

Unfortunately, he was shot outside one of his stores in Los Angeles. I turned on the TV the other day and saw his funeral. Thousands upon thousands of people were paying their respects to him: black people, white people; rich, poor, gay, and straight people; Asian, Jewish, Muslim, and Christian people; Bloods and Crips and Latino gang members ... all were gathered together, crying, holding hands, and patting the cars as they came by. They stood together, holding up pictures of Nipsey.

Nipsey left a legacy, but not a lot of people knew what he was all about until after he died. He worked hard to become the most elite version of himself. Even after his death, his music continues to impact the lives of thousands of people in his hometown and millions more throughout the world. Nothing says that you can't do the same thing, but it'll never happen if you return to "fine."

You were put on this planet to become the most elite version of yourself. But somewhere along the way, you sold your soul to the force of average and settled for comfortable. Now you're so comfortable that you've convinced yourself that when you do one wild thing, you've stepped outside your comfort zone. So you return to "fine" for six months with no desire to shake up your life.

Since we've done the work to define your comfort zones

clearly, why would you return to any of those zones, knowing that nothing good comes from living there?

Let me rephrase that.

Plenty of good comes from the comfort zone, but nothing great comes from it.

You're reading this book because you desire greatness. This is the G Code, AKA the code to greatness—it's not the code to "fine," not the code to average, not the code to being a victim of the force of average. Remember that, as you get deeper into this book, the G Code is the code to greatness. That's what we're striving for.

If we want to achieve greatness, we have to understand what "good" is.

We've defined what's comfortable and "fine" for you. And we've defined what greatness is.

I know that when you did the visualization exercise, you felt the difference between *how* you're living your life and *how you want to* live your life. When you opened your eyes, you may have cried. You may have realized that you're so far behind what you could have been at this point of your life that you shed tears. I've seen this happen in plenty of audiences—people with tears running down their cheeks because they finally take the time to see who they can be and what their existence can be like. They see where they are and all the work ahead of them. They see time wasted and how they haven't loved themselves. They learn that they are where they are because they haven't given a damn and have treated themselves like garbage. *Of course* it's enough to make you cry. I interpret your emotions as a good thing—you want to make a change.

The good news is that you're only a few steps away from greatness. Each year contains 365 days. If you take a few steps per day and compound the years, that's thousands upon thousands of steps that you can use to move forward in your life.

Every step, every day starts with following the G Code. I'm going to give you the steps to follow every single day to make power moves and get and stay focused on what matters most so you can become the most elite version of yourself.

I did this exercise years ago, and I cried because I was falling really fucking short of who I was supposed to be.

I had anger issues. I had mental baggage. I was easily distracted. But two years ago, when I started sticking to the G Code, I stepped into the most elite version of myself. Today, I am that person I envisioned. I'm still not perfect because of that carrot at the end of the stick I'm always chasing, but I'm damn sure better than what I *even imagined I could be* two years ago.

The same transformation will happen for you in two years if you stick to the G Code. Do not be distracted. Do not return to "fine."

Congratulations on reading this far and keeping your focus— those who dare to read the entire *G Code* become part of an unstoppable movement. Keep reading and you will join the force, making power moves working against the force of average.

4

THE FIGHT TO FOCUS

The theme of this book is about getting focused. In a world of constant ADHD diagnoses—where teachers constantly tell us that we can't pay attention, where society demands us to be a certain way that we're not genetically predispositioned to be —this book gives you the tools you need.

Everything you need to stay your course is here on these pages.

If you use what I am teaching you, you won't have to rely on medication, a special diet, or anything else. This book has the tools that you need every day to get and stay focused. We all need these tools because we are in a fight to stay focused every day of our lives.

The force of average tries to distract us all day, every day. The more it distracts us, the more it wins. It even keeps score. It knows when you're winning, and that's when it hits you extra hard. We have to understand that we're in a fight, and the only way we can win that fight is by staying focused. If we get distracted, we lose.

You have to hold your focus if you want to be successful—

that's why, in the next few pages, I'm going to teach you my proven system for maintaining focus. It's worked for me. It's worked for my employees. It's worked for my clients. It's worked for my friends. It's even worked for my children. And it's so simple that all you have to do is follow the steps I lay out.

Follow my lead and trust that the information I'm going to share with you comes from real experience. I didn't read it in a medical textbook, and I didn't hear it from a friend of a friend. I've used the G Code to create the life I wanted. And it works, because I'm living that life right now. I am living, breathing proof that your life can be different, just like mine—despite the fact that doctors and teachers insisted I needed to be on ADHD medications. If you're in the same boat, you can change your life, too. Your life can be exactly as you envisioned it to be when you did the exercise where you imagined the most elite version of yourself.

I took medication for hyperactivity and focus issues from the age of 11 until I was 27 years old. The doctors gave me a product called Ritalin, which was the OG ADHD drug. When I was a kid, ADHD and ADD didn't have a name. If you weren't paying attention in class (which was fucking boring to me), the doctors gave you focus drugs that were basically methamphetamine in a pill form so that you would shut the fuck up.

If you look up the description of Ritalin or any of the other types of drugs they prescribe for ADHD or ADD, you'll find out that they're pharmaceutically made methamphetamine. Of course these pills aren't made in a meth lab. But they *are* made in a lab, and the ingredients make up the same damn concoction as meth.

After Ritalin, my doctors moved me onto Cylert and Norpramin. Because of the side effects of the methamphetamine in the drugs, I didn't have the desire to play football and basketball anymore.

Doped out of my mind, I would sit in my room and zone out on video games for long-ass hours on end. Time slipped by because I'd be high as hell on the pills that my parents and the doctors made me take. Since I didn't have the energy to go out and play sports, and because my body felt weird from the side effects of the drug, I would play video games or listen to music endlessly. I especially loved reading the lyrics on the inside of CD covers.

Then I started trying other drugs. Understandably, I thought, *Hell, I'm already on a drug, what's another one?* After swallowing down Ritalin for a while, I moved on to crushing and snorting Adderall. The more I took, the higher I got. Eventually, that high didn't do anything for me, so I tried more drugs. Then, *that* wasn't enough, so I just kept going. By my 20s, I had a full-blown methamphetamine addiction.

I'd been using meth for six months, but I was still productive and making money. I wasn't out partying or doing too much weird stuff, but I had a full-blown addiction. People say that marijuana is a gateway drug, but the gateway drug for me was what the doctors prescribed.

I had been so deep into using that I couldn't acknowledge there was a problem. Then, one day it hit me, *Oh shit, I'm on drugs.* Shortly after that, I realized, *I've got to get the fuck off them.* I kicked meth and got back on Adderall. Then I weaned myself off that. I have not touched the stuff since 2009.

To get clean, I had to understand what focus was. When you take Adderall, Ritalin, or other drugs, it weakens your subconscious ability to channel your focus. You can compare it to steroids or any other synthetic injection.

When I was on drugs, people around me had no idea I was taking them. The only person who knew was my dealer, so when I wanted to get clean, I had a problem.

As I was getting clean, I had to make it seem like there was nothing different about me. I couldn't act differently. I couldn't be a different person. No one could discover the big lie I was hiding.

Since the drugs made me into a focused person, I had to maintain that focus. I started on a journey to beat my addiction without anyone knowing.

In 2009, I read books, went to seminars, and watched videos.

You'll note that was approximately 10 years before the time of my writing this book.

On my journey to get clean, I found something called Rhodiola root.

One day, I was talking to a friend I hadn't seen in a couple of months. He said, "Hey, man, you look good. Did you gain a few pounds?" Since I had gone off the drugs, I was eating and sleeping. I replied, "Yeah, I quit taking Adderall. I've been taking it pretty much my whole life, and I just stopped." Then my friend said, "You know what? I'm an Amway distributor. I can help you with a supplement. You'll never need or feel like you need Adderall again to pay attention." Immediately, I thought, *Oh, here we go with this shit.*

I let him talk anyway.

He said, "Amway has something called Rhodiola root. It's great for people who have ADHD." That sounded exactly like what I was looking for. I found out it was about $40 a bottle. The price was in reach. I had to try it.

So I went to the building where my friend told me to go, signed up, and bought the Rhodiola root. I took it, and lo and behold, it allowed me to focus. It gave my brain the nutrients that I needed to pay attention. I've now been taking Rhodiola root since that first day I bought a bottle. You can go to Amazon.com right now and get it for yourself. There are all sorts of different varieties and dosages, so you can figure out what will work for you. I'm of the school of thought that the higher the dosage, the better. But no matter what strength you buy, give it a go. You can even combine the root with other supplements. Keep reading, because I am about to tell you what other supplements I take.

Two of the supplements I take can be found on Amazon.

Do a search for Focus Pills. You can get a bottle of Focus Pills for about $29.

Next, search for Optify Mushrooms and get yourself some of those, too.

After Amazon, go to a site called 1stphorm.com. Check out the M-FACTOR pill, then do a search for FULL-MEGA, which is the brand name for their omega-3 fish oil.

I take a total of five pills every day. One of each: Rhodiola Root, Focus Pills, Optify Mushrooms, FULL-MEGA, and M-FACTOR. These supplements will give your body the building blocks and nutrition it needs. I've tried other supplements like Alpha BRAIN and MasterBrain, but these five are what's worked best for me.

Your body composition may be different than mine, but it's worth it to try these supplements. Supplements are not designed to work right away, so when you start taking them, stick with it for at least a month. The goal is to get the nutrients delivered to your body. Once you ingest the nutrients, you're ready to work out.

It's a fact that your brain needs a workout as much as your body. You know that if you want to strengthen your muscles, you have to work out. The same is true of your mind. You have to work it out consistently for it to grow stronger and more focused.

Vitamins are like steroids for your mind. They help you strengthen your focus. But it's not enough to simply strengthen your focus, you've also got to exercise your brain. That's why

I've developed mindset exercises for you to use every day that will help you improve your ability to focus.

First, I want you to set aside five minutes every single day to work on your brain. Put it on your calendar. Don't worry about scheduling the same time every day. You can vary the times. You simply need to block out five minutes at some point during the day every day.

I don't care what the average guru or "expert" on this subject tells you. I'm telling you that you only need five minutes to create meaningful mindset traction. Bolder people can go for ten minutes, but to get your feet wet, you just need that initial five minutes. That's the great thing about this book. I'm giving you practical advice that you can put into action and use to change your life. And it's not brain surgery.

1. Take the pills on the list.
2. Do the exercises.
3. Follow the pattern.
4. Repeat.

That's the G Code—the premise of this entire book.

Once you've carved out those five minutes, dedicate them to meditation. If we're faced with a million decisions every day and 4,000 plus distractions, we're experiencing constant stress and anxiety. That's why we need to take five minutes to silence everything that's going on in our heads.

If you want to meditate longer than five minutes, that's fine, but let's not set outrageous goals for ourselves. We don't have to 10X our goals. All we have to do is set up a practical plan and stick to it. I know you can do this because all you have to do is take one step every single day. And you can meditate for these five minutes a day anywhere, anytime. You can be at your desk or on your couch, I don't care. Just make sure that it's quiet around you. So carve out the time, find a comfortable space, set a timer, and close your eyes.

Before you go off on a meditation tangent, let me share with you how I meditate and what works for me. I keep it very uncomplicated, and because it works for me, I know it will work for you.

I'm no meditation expert, but I know our brains are constantly working. Your brain never takes a minute to relax. When you can get your brain to relax from doing 100 million jobs at once and get it focused on only doing one job, it builds up the ability to stay focused on one thing at a time. This is the meditation conditioning that I want you to do every day.

So many people can't get shit accomplished in their lives because they're trying to do 50 million things at once. Even though you might feel like you're being productive as hell, I hate to burst your bubble, but it's highly unlikely that you're able to multitask effectively.

If you ask most people how they get things done, the answer you'll hear most frequently is that they're multitaskers. But did you know that it's been scientifically proven that only 2.5% of society can actually multitask?[2] By this, I mean multitask well. This is because the force of average is fighting us.

When we multitask, the force of average is winning. Remember, it wins when your focus is fragmented all over the place.

The force of average has us convinced that we can do something that we actually can't. It wants us to dilute our focus on different tasks, because when we do that, we don't accomplish any of those tasks very well, not even one. But you'll think that you're checking things off your list and doing a good job. That's what the force of average wants you to think.

When we do a mediocre job, we can't dominate, can we? We can't do all of the things we're trying to do at once because, in order to get anything done, we have to channel all of our energies toward a singular focus.

But how do we accomplish getting and staying focused?

Through meditating five minutes every day.

To start, set a five-minute timer on your phone. Then, close your eyes and get into a comfortable position. Lie down with a pillow underneath your head, or sit with your legs crossed casually. You don't have to be in a Zen, douchey-looking, weird contortion with beads around your neck and your fingers touching your thumbs.

You don't need a lot of preparation, either.

When you meditate, keep it simple.

Once you're comfortable, relax and let everything go for a second. Take your mind off your problems. For the moment, forget about your issues. While you're in this position, think about one thing and one thing only—your breath.

Think about how it feels as you take air in through your nose and your nasal cavity, then as it travels down your throat and into your lungs, expanding your lungs, your ribcage, and all of your bronchial tubes.

On the exhale, think about the air traveling back up your throat and out your mouth. Focus on how it feels to inhale and exhale for the next five minutes. Think about nothing but your breathing. Don't count the breaths. Don't worry about whether you're doing it the right way or not.

Every time you catch yourself thinking about something else besides your breath, bring your attention back to your breathing. You want to think about your breath and your breath only.

Nothing else matters besides your breathing because nobody and nothing will miss five minutes from you. You get five minutes of pure dedication to train your brain to focus on one task only—your breath.

During these five minutes, when you're focusing on your

breath, the force of average will try to convince you that your problems are real and that you need to stop what you're doing. It will tell you lies that you can't be away from work that long. You need to be aware of this so you can anticipate it and overcome it. This is just a little game that the force of average plays with your brain because it doesn't want you to strengthen your focus muscles. Once you have strong focus muscles, you become an unstoppable human being, and that does not bode well for the force of average.

Since we're likely part of the 98% who can't multitask, we must strengthen our ability to focus by exercising the muscles that strengthen our focus. When we do this, each one of us becomes a focused individual.

During these five minutes that you're taking for yourself, breathe in, and as you do, trace every step that your breath takes throughout your entire body and circulatory system. In and out. Inhale and exhale. Repeat. For five minutes, focus only on your breath. Every time you start thinking about something else, remind yourself that you're supposed to think about your breath only. Then, once again, get focused on your breath.

Every time your mind tries to stray, remind it nicely that it's supposed to be focused on your breath, then redirect your focus.

Five minutes of meditation a day will change your life in 30 days. You'll get better at focusing each time you do it. Once you get better, you'll want to see how long you can focus. I'm up to 10 minutes a day, but I started off with five minutes. That was all I needed when I started—and it's all you'll need, too.

Our brains are fucking busy, and if we don't give them a break, I believe we can make them susceptible to Alzheimer's and other related brain issues. If you don't take the time to retrain your brain to focus, you're going to be in trouble as you get older. When you do things by the G Code, the older you get, the more focused you'll get, the more you'll accomplish, and the more you'll win.

At this point, we've covered supplementation and meditation. Now it's time to add in time management skills.

Time management is key to helping you accomplish what you want to do.

During the day, we know that we have to focus. We know that we have responsibilities to attend to. That's why I live and die by a schedule.

As the head of a company, I don't have a boss. Even when I was a salesman, because I was the top producer, I didn't have anyone breathing over my shoulder. In whatever position I've held, I've had to create accountability. I did this, and continue to do this, by keeping to a schedule to make the most of my time. I manage my time correctly every day, and you need to do the same. We'll go into more depth later in Chapter 12, but you'll soon learn that time management is a huge part of the G Code.

Now that I've given you some of the tools you need to focus (the supplements and meditation exercise), it's time to identify what to focus on.

In a later chapter of this book, we're going to break down your focus into four areas that we call the G Code. These are the four areas of your life where you will focus on getting wins every single day. So keep reading to get the scoop on these areas as well as my secrets for keeping a highly efficient calendar.

For now, let's get back to the topic of focus. So many people have been told at a young age that they can't focus. They've been diagnosed with ADD and other attention or learning disorders, but the truth is, we all have it within us to focus. We just have to take a few extra supplements to help us out, and we have to flex that focus muscle for five minutes every single day. When you take these measures, they add up. You become more determined. When you push your power to focus, then your focus transforms into resolve, and your resolve helps you see your mission through to completion.

Most people won't focus on one task and complete it because they're scared of completion. They're afraid that what they are making is going to suck.

If I create an offer or product and present it to the public, and they tell me that it sucks by not buying it, I have to deal with those consequences. I need to decide if I'm going to keep working on it, trying to make it better, or if I'm going to believe the marketplace that's telling me that I have a terrible product.

This is another reason why most people are so distracted by so many things at once. They're scared to finish one thing because of their fear of judgment; it's easier and less painful to turn their efforts to their next project. But part of being focused on what you need to do is finishing the task you started. If the marketplace doesn't like it, don't just start something else. Tweak your original product and make it better. Use the feedback to your benefit. Plenty of today's products are amazing, but they didn't start that way. They had to be improved upon before anyone paid them any positive attention.

Amazon is a prime example. Amazon started off selling books. But we all know that, compared to marketplace consumers as a whole, there are not that many people that buy books. Jeff Bezos saw that there was an opportunity to do more than sell books. He also saw that the market wanted more, so he went back to the drawing board and made improvements until the Goliath that is today's Amazon was born.

It's true that when you tweak a product to make it right, the world will judge you. This is going to happen no matter what you decide to do. But it doesn't matter. Your job is to stay focused no matter what. If your product isn't well-received or the launch doesn't go right, your job is to make the adjustments needed and then relaunch. If you do this enough times, you'll end up with a product that everyone loves.

Today, everyone loves Amazon. They sell everything because they can. They've capitalized on their hard work through repeatedly perfecting their offers.

The key to stepping into your full potential is focusing on one thing and one thing only. But I don't mean that you just focus on meditation, for example. No. I mean that you apply what you have learned. For example, you apply *how to focus during meditation* to the rest of your life.

Focus on achieving greatness in your life. That's why you're reading this book. You want to experience greatness. I want you to experience it, too. That's why I'm breaking down some of the most complex, hard-to-understand truths and simplifying them so that anybody can grasp them and use them to their advantage.

We're focused on greatness, and that's what the G Code is all about.

The G Code covers the four areas in our lives that we must be focused on if we're going to be great at anything. Later on in the book, you'll learn exactly what those four areas are and how to maintain your focus on them. You'll learn the specific strategies and exact daily routines that have made such a significant difference in all the areas of my life that matter—not just in business or the amount of money I make, but in the love that I have at home and the love that I share with my friends. I'm feeling the difference of reduced stress and anxiety from society. Since I've been following the code, everything in my life has changed. That's why I want to share it with you. You've picked up this book for a reason, and that reason is to make your life different.

As you read this book and learn about the G Code, your job as a steward of the code is to make sure that you pass this knowledge on to somebody else who needs to hear it. Passing this knowledge along is crucial because there are plenty of people out there who are longing for change just like you. You know you want to help them because it feels so incredible to help people step into their own unique greatness. The G Code is a movement. It will roll from one person to the next, improving lives along the way.

In the coming pages, you'll learn that the superhuman power to focus is the foundation of everything. This is why I come back to it time and time again. This is a superpower that you must practice often; it's the superpower that can help create miracles.

5

CLARITY IS POWER

I n the previous chapter, we talked about what it means to try to maintain focus in the war of distraction that we're in every day.

We're constantly being distracted by the force of average. But when we understand that focus is power, we understand the power of focus.

In this chapter, we're going to talk about gaining clarity. If power is the end result, and focus is the bridge to get there, the very foundation that holds the bridge up on each side is clarity.

A few years ago, I was watching a news special like *Dateline*. In a survey of the entire world, a reporter had come to the conclusion that people from Denmark use the least amount of words daily. Apparently, Danish people don't speak very much. One of the examples they gave on the show was of a gentleman who was sitting next to another gentleman on a subway.

Now, in Texas, if we were on a train, bus, or subway, we would simply look at the person next to us, and if we needed to climb over their legs, we would say, "Excuse me."

In New York, in my experience, people might look at the person sitting next to them and say, "Get out of the way."

Well, in Denmark, it seems that people shuffle their newspaper as a signal that they're about to move, and the person next to them automatically moves their legs out of the way. In other words, people in Denmark communicate nonverbally. When the reporter learned this, he was intrigued and dug a little deeper. He went on to discover that freedom of speech is different in Scandinavian countries than it is in America, the reporter's country of origin.

Freedom of speech and misuse of speech in Scandinavian countries can be prosecuted by the government. Because of this, Danish people tend to speak less so their words can't be used against them.

I watched that show decades ago, but it's always stuck with me.

Scandinavians use very few words and vague language so that they're not held accountable for their speech, only for their actions. They don't risk using words that someone might hold against them.

We take advantage of all the words we can use in America because we have free speech. We can say whatever the fuck we want whenever the fuck we feel like saying it. But it's not that way everywhere else.

But now, even in America, the definitions of words are changing. Words that used to have a specific meaning have been replaced with words that are vague. We're following in the Danish people's footsteps.

You might wonder why we would want to change our language to become vaguer. I'm no expert on Scandinavian governments or the American government, either. But I do understand that there is a difference between having intentions you can absolutely prove—especially in a court of law—and arriving at a place or result without intention.

I'll give you a better idea of what I mean.

Let's say you were driving down the street and dropped your phone. You reached down to pick up your phone and, in doing so, ran up the curve and fatally injured a person. You're going to be in serious trouble, but it was an accident, so you're probably going to get off without any jail time—you'll just be stressed out and have to live with what you've done for the rest of your life.

Let's take that same scenario and discuss intention.

This time, you're driving down the street when you see somebody who owes you $10,000. That person is cheating with your significant other and beating up your kids. And it's the same somebody who's been bullying and stealing from you your entire life. You swerve up on the sidewalk and run over that motherfucker. The end result is the same. A person is fatally injured. The difference between you doing a life sentence for running somebody over and getting off for having an accident is your intention.

The force of average understands the intentions behind your words, and it's programming us more and more every single day to become less intentional and clear when we speak. When we speak vaguely, our subconscious can't understand what's going on. Because it can't process what we mean, our intentions don't make it into our conscious mind to create actual, living thoughts. When we use vague language, we turn words like "bad" into meaning "good" and "good" into meaning "bad." You can see how this would be confusing to your conscious mind.

We use words that don't make any sense, and their meaning becomes vaguer. Then we use those words in our daily language. Next, we invent new words and assign them meanings that don't matter—words like "crunk." The dictionary even includes these words because we use them regularly. This keeps the cycle going and encourages more use.

Here's another example:

When referring to our partner in life, we used to say "significant other." Now we say "bae." Do you see the difference? It might not seem like a big deal, but when we said "significant other," we meant that person was a significant part of our lives. They were the significant other half. Now we say "bae," which can mean fucking anything. "That's my bae." "That's my boo." Our language becomes vaguer and vaguer. "Boo" doesn't mean they're significant. "Bae" doesn't mean they're significant. Does that name mean that they're your girlfriend? Your wife? Your husband? Does it mean they're some dude you're banging?

People use less intentional language because they want to accept less responsibility. On social media, the people who use this kind of language are hateful trolls hiding behind fake profiles. That's the power of vagueness. Trolls know that if they use particular words, they can't be held accountable for their intentions.

The reason I share this with you is that this is just one area of our lives where we're fighting for clarity every single day.

A long time ago, when I started training business owners on social media courses, I'd instruct people on how to run their social media to attract people. I would say that we have to appear intentional on social media because everybody else shows up and just starts scrolling the newsfeed and letting social media *happen* around them. If we want to make a difference, we have to be intentional about what we're doing. We're not there for entertainment. As business people, we're there for the money.

I feel the same way about life on this planet. When most people are born, they let life happen to them. Their parents manage their existence and make decisions that directly affect their lives for years on end. They go to the schools that they're appointed to and get used to life happening to them for 18 to 20 years. As you're growing up, you're at the mercy of your parents. You're at the mercy of your family. You're at the mercy of your siblings, teachers, surroundings, and your ability to move around in the world. Life happens around you before you can come of age and take part in it.

We get used to life being this way. But when we get past that 18- to 20-year-old mark, or whenever we recognize our circumstances, we start getting intentional. Some of us need to get intentional earlier than others. I was almost 15 when I left home, so I had to get serious about what I wanted to do then. But no matter what age we are, at some point, we wake up and live our lives intentionally. We intentionally go out to find our dream job. We intentionally start the company we've wanted to start for years. We intentionally know who we want to fall in love with. We intentionally build the empire we know we were destined to build.

Those of us who have intentions and who live intentionally also receive the consequences of those intentions. As we all know, consequences can have a negative connotation. But the truth is, there are good consequences more often than bad consequences. It's just that we're taught to ignore the good consequences. Even if more positive things are happening in our lives than negative things, we get focused on the negative, and that's all we can see.

In this chapter, we're going to get clear on how to see the good consequences. We're going to achieve clarity because clarity leads to focus. When you're clear, you *know* what to focus on. And we know that focus is power. That means clarity is the very foundation that will lead to us finding power in ourselves. So let's get specific with our lives. Let's get specific with our intentions. In doing so, we will create clarity.

Here's another example:

In 2014, I was facing a devastating divorce.

Our divorce came about after a phone call with my soon to be ex-wife. At the end of the conversation, I thought I had hung up the phone. My wife also thought she had hung up the phone, but neither of us had. As a result, I overheard a conversation of all the mean things she and her friend said about me.

After we said, "Love you," and "Love you, too, bye." I thought the phone was on the hook. Instead, I overheard her telling her friend how she was using me for money and how my parents were wealthy—which was far from true. She had a situation concocted in her head that was so different from reality. When I realized she was just using me and *she realized* I'd heard that conversation, we divorced.

My second wife divorced me while I was in prison, which was also quite the blow.

My third divorce had a new twist.

When wife number three and I divorced, I had a two-year-old son, Jackson, the absolute apple of my eye. As I write this book, he's now eight-years-old. Since day one, I have loved that kid with everything in my heart. I set out in life to stay married to his mother because I didn't want my son, or any of my kids, to grow up in a divorced household. When that didn't happen, and I got divorced from his mom, I felt like I was failing at another one of my goals. I also knew that I didn't want to grow old alone.

We divorced anyway, and I told myself I wasn't good at marriage. Then I started wondering why that was. *How had I fucked up three marriages? How had it come to this?* Maybe I could blame wife number one for talking in that derogatory way about me. Maybe I could blame wife number two because, after all, I was in prison. When I divorced wife number three, I did some internal reflection. I then realized that even if unforeseen consequences and issues arose that caused the divorce, I was still attracting the kind of person into my life that I could never have a lasting relationship with.

I had to get clear on what I wanted.

When I look back at those three ex-wives, I realize that none of them were alike—not in personality and not in looks. In every single way you can think of, they were completely different. I mean no disrespect to those women, but I was unintentionally bouncing from one female who would accept me and tell me she loved me to another female who would accept me and tell me she loved me.

In 2014, I decided to fight that force of average in my life and got very specific about dialing in to the type of person that I wanted to spend the rest of my life with. She was a woman into exercise and yoga. I wanted to have three kids, not just one, so she had to be willing to do that. I designed everything, from the way that this woman looked to her personality to the way that she acted to the activities that she would do every single day. I wrote everything down and called my list My Perfect Spouse. I knew she would have all those qualities, some of which were pretty hard to believe. After three failed marriages, I was aware of exactly what I didn't want, so it wasn't that hard to put it all down on paper.

Fast forward to September of 2014. I was visiting Arizona, shooting a TV show (that never aired by the way, so don't get all excited on me). I needed a date for the show, so I went on a dating site, signed up, and swiped through trying to connect with somebody. My soon to be wife, Amy, was one of those people I connected with, but I missed our planned date on that trip. A month later, on the next trip, when I did another episode of the show, Amy was my date. We had been talking via text and FaceTime for about a month. She picked me up from the airport. We instantly fell for each other. The next thing you know, she'd spent one weekend in Texas, and I'd spent one weekend in Arizona.

As I got to know her over the next few months, I thought back to when I'd written the My Perfect Spouse list. The more I thought about it, the more traits I checked off that Amy has—mostly the extremely high standards that I never thought I would see in my partner.

One day, I handed Amy a write-up—essentially my business plan for marriage—that included what my perfect spouse would be like. Amy said, "Oh, you wrote this about me recently, huh?"

But I had written it months before we'd even met. That's the power of clarity. I got clear on what I wanted in my life, and now I'm married to the perfect person—all because I took a moment and clarified my vision. I didn't want to accept somebody who was willing to fuck me, share a house with me, or someone who was even willing to love me. I found someone who respects me. Someone who respects herself. Someone who has an extreme amount of confidence. Someone who's self-supportive. I have Amy in my life because I got clear on what I wanted and what I didn't want. That's what I mean by clarity is power.

So many people go through divorce because they weren't clear on who or what they wanted in their relationship in the first place. In the same way, most people hate their jobs because they weren't clear on who or what they wanted from a boss or corporation. They just applied to the company looking for a means to an end, and when they were hired, they accepted that they would get a paycheck every two weeks.

We're very vague, and when our subconscious is trying to process our words, there's a ton of ambiguity that makes absolutely no sense. When we just let life happen to us, it hinders us. This is why things don't work out. We put no thought into what we do or what we want for ourselves.

In the meantime, those of us who get intentional and create

clarity in every area of our lives—from how we want to live each day to how we want to eat to what our exercise regimen is—experience peace. When you get clear on what you want in your spouse, children, corporation, employees, manager, leader, friend, higher power, or any other area of your life, you create a calmness that makes you unstoppable. Calmness allows you to focus.

In short, you're distracted when you're vague and focused when you're clear.

We now know that focus is the most powerful superhuman weapon on the planet. Therefore, clarity equals power.

It's time to create clarity in your life, so here's my challenge to you:

Take the next full hour and work on the following exercise.

This is your hour to get clear. Get clear on what you want from your family. Get clear on what you want from your corporation. Get clear on what you want from yourself. How do you want to eat? How do you want to live? How do you want to look? Get clear on these core areas of your life so you can be focused on what you need to do—so you can see your way to your goals.

You've heard of people who've put a picture of a Lamborghini on their computer desktop so they could see it every day, right? Every moment of every day, as they looked at that picture, they got clear that they wanted that Lamborghini. Then, one day, that dream came true; they could buy their Lamborghini. That's because they were so clear about what they wanted. When you get clear on what you want, you can take the actionable steps that will get you exactly that.

This is how you step into power.

Take the next hour and create clarity. Write down what you want in your life. Get into Evernote. Grab a pen, notepad, or however you want to record what you want. Voice text it. That's fine. It doesn't matter how you do it. It's your time to create absolute clarity in your life.

Remember, this book will do you absolutely no good if you don't take action on what you're reading.

This book is not only for you to learn about what the G Code is. It should also allow you to *live* for what you want in every area of your life, so take a pause for the next hour and create clarity in your life. I'll see you in 60 minutes.

6

THE LEVELS

So far in this book you've learned that there's an algorithm called the force of average and that this force is after you. You know we have to fight it with focus. You also know that the way we gain focus—our power—is through clarity. From this, we can determine that clarity equals power.

Now I'm going to give you a clear and precise way to determine where and how to level up in your life. The fact that you're reading a book like this means that you're trying to improve yourself. You *want* to level up, so let's define what that means.

We hear the phrase "level up" all the time—especially if we're in particular industries or work in entrepreneurship. "Level Up" companies and even "Next Level Productions" exist. Hell, I order their T-shirts. But did you know the phrase "level up" is actually a deception originating from the force of average?

We hear people say, "I want to level up," and they *think* they're focused on leveling up, but what do they mean? What does leveling up mean to you? If we know that clarity is power, have you clarified what leveling up means? How do you know that you're not currently leveling up? It sounds confusing, but there's a better way to explain the concept of leveling up that's easy for everyone to understand.

We can use the analogy of playing a video game.

When you're playing a video game and on a specific level, before you can move up to the next level, you have to fight the guys or characters. If it's a racing game, you need to get over the finish line. No matter the kind of game, you have to complete tasks and reach specific goals before you can get to the end of each level. Once you get to the end of the level, the game gets harder than ever. You keep moving up through the levels, trying to defeat the big boss at the end of each level.

When I was a kid, my parents bought my sister and me a Nintendo system. We played *Kung Fu*. In *Kung Fu*, you move along a stage and fight the guys that come at you. Now, remember, this is the original Nintendo. These guys would advance, and you would sweep kick them, leg kick them, punch them, and jump over them. When you had fought and won against enough of them, you'd get to the end of the level and meet the big boss. That dude had some skills, and he was harder to beat than anyone else. But until you beat the big boss, you couldn't go to the next level.

Life is a lot like that, isn't it? Many of us want to go to the next level, but when we're faced with the big boss, we turn around, tuck our tail between our legs, and run off like cowards. We tell ourselves that we want to solve problems, but we're not clear on what problems we can and can't solve. We're not clear on whether we're a problem solver or not. Maybe leveling up sounds cool, but we don't want to do what it takes to get there.

And so, we go through life with this vagueness surrounding us.

This ends right here. I'm going to teach you what it means

and what it takes to level up. I'm going to give you a point system so you can see if people around you are leveling up as well. You need to know this is because their levels affect your levels.

This point system requires a mathematical equation, but as long as you can count to 16, you'll have no problem. To give you a brief overview, there are four levels, and you will have the ability to score between 1 to 4 points in each level, reaching a maximum of 16 points.

The four areas we're going to concentrate on correspond with the four areas of the G Code: Gratitude (mindset), Genetics (health and fitness), Grind (business), and Group (family).

Let's start with Gratitude. The whole point is to start your day off with gratitude. We wake up in the morning, we check our phones, we check social media ... and it's calamity, right?

Employees call in sick. People email you and text you and send you DMs overnight, and it's rarely good news. So you wake up first thing in the morning and you check out your phone, and it starts making you ungrateful for your situation.

A lot of people say that they're not a morning person, but the reason they're not a morning person is they're not grateful to be alive—they don't have a grateful mindset. They haven't experienced that gratitude of being able to wake up. There are millions of people who go to sleep at night who don't wake up in the morning, every single day. We have to start our day off being grateful that we're alive. That's why gratitude is number one. Because if we're not grateful and if we don't program ourselves to be grateful first, then the rest of the stuff in the G Code won't matter. As a matter of fact, if you're not grateful, then the rest of the stuff in your life won't matter because if you're not grateful for what you have now, it doesn't matter how much more stuff you get, you won't be grateful for it either. The true balance in life that we're seeking is the balance between being grateful for what we have while being in pursuit of what's next in our lives.

The Second Level in the G Code is Genetics, which is all about health and fitness.

We've gotten to the point in America where we clap for people who are out of shape and shame people who have worked their entire lives to look good and be healthy. It's the weirdest damn thing I've ever seen, but I know why it's happening; it's the force of average trying to distract us and make us unhealthy. It tells us that it's okay to be in our comfort zone. It's okay to be overweight. It's okay not to look like an athlete. It's okay if you don't want to work out. It's okay if you just want to put on yoga pants but never do a yoga class in your life. That's okay.

But it's not okay for people who don't want to be average. It might be okay for the people who want to die early of type 2 diabetes or heart disease, or whatever disease they'll get from not taking care of themselves. But it's not okay for the rest of us who are trying to be great. You fall into this category because *you are reading this book.*

If we want to strive to be better physically, we have to assign ourselves a ranking of where we are now. We have to assess our standing just like we'll be doing on the other three levels. When we do this, we'll know whether we are or aren't at a point in our lives where we need to level up.

When we look at our body types, we have to ask ourselves, *Are we out of shape?* And if so, *To what degree?* At certain times in my life, I've thought, *You've gotta hit it harder.* I haven't slacked on my fitness, but sometimes you have to do a little more to maintain or knock off those extra few pounds. I've been consistently working on my body and going to the gym multiple times per week since I was 19 years old. I'm a high-stress, high-anxiety guy, so working out allows me to get rid of some of my energy and release a lot of my nervousness. It'll do the same for you.

I don't have a story about being a big guy who was massively overweight and then lost all of it. My story is 20 years of unyielding consistency. I don't take any prescriptions, and when I go to the doctor, they tell me I'm 100% healthy. The force of average has tried to kill me at least five different times, but I'm still fucking breathing. I don't have the best diet, and I don't even look the best, but I'm healthy. I believe that's because I keep working on my genetics.

Regardless of what your physical state is, you have to understand where you fall in the range. If you're out of shape, to what degree are you out of shape? Are you overweight, or are you just average, like most Americans, when it comes to being out of shape? If you're overweight, make today the day that you say, "It's time to level up and become average." You don't have to go to level four. Simply make the commitment to get to level two, *then* you can worry about level three. After that, you can worry about level four. You just want to get started, so set your sights on level two and reaching an average state.

If you're an average man living in America, according to the CDC, your waist is over 39 inches. If you're a man with a waist over 39 inches, but you're not 7-foot fucking tall with a 10-foot cock, then it's time to level up to level two and get in shape. You can take many actions to get in shape, like taking a CrossFit class or going to Orangetheory or kickboxing boot camp. It doesn't matter what you choose to do to get into shape, just make sure it's challenging. Don't get a membership at the local gym and promise to go there and bench press for 30 minutes three times a week. That's fucking stupid. That shit worked in the 70s because people didn't know what the fuck they were doing. Back then, they didn't have Google.

The point is to find yourself something that will challenge

you, whether it's a spin class or you cycle with a bunch of other spandex-wearing people. Take a yoga class or do SoulCycle. Try out Body Fitness or Body Machine. These are just a few suggestions to get you started. You can research and find more options for yourself, but no matter what you decide, there's a challenging activity that will give you something to set your sights on. Once you decide what you're going to do, zero in on the numbers and measurements you need to reach to meet your goal.

The other alternative is to get a trainer and commit to them. I've had a trainer for the last year, and I'm committed to him, whether I like it or not.

If you're in shape, the next level you want to hit is to be ripped and reach single-digit body fat.

In the area of genetics (health and fitness), we can define physicality on levels such as out-of-shape, average-body-type, in-shape, or absolutely-ripped.

Level 3 or The Third G is Grind. Your level of grind determines your financial status.

If you think about it, our financial standing makes up varying levels of poor, average, rich, and wealthy.

As it pertains to your financial status, you might be dreaming of the day you can level up. My friend, Matt Manero, runs a company called Commercial Fleet Financing. He wrote a book called *You Need More Money*. Matt's a great guy. I have a tremendous amount of respect for him. He spoke at one of our seminars and said, "Life begins at $100,000." My ears perked up when I heard him say that, and I thought, *I like the way this guy thinks*.

From the stage, Matt said, "Life gets pretty good around $250,000 a year." He went on, "You become unstoppable at half a million a year. And if you make a million+ a year, you get rich-rich. You become wealthy."

Take a moment to think about that.

What financial level are you on right now? Many of you have sold your dreams and desires for a $60,000 to $70,000 salary working 60 to 70 hours a week for someone you hate. You say you want to level up, but you're riddled with fear, crippled by debt, and don't know what the fuck to do with your life.

Listen, I understand. But life doesn't begin in America until you're making six figures a year. If you're married, you don't get to say, "Combined, we make six figures a year." That doesn't count. I'm talking about you alone. Understand, I'm not here to bash people who aren't making a specific amount of money. I'm not here to bash people with a salaried job. I'm simply saying that you're missing out on an important part of life by not earning that amount of money.

It's so easy to make money these days. Forget whatever excuses just went through your head as you read that. It's so easy, that you have no excuse. Guys like Gary V. are buying My Little Ponies and flipping them on eBay, making an extra couple hundred dollars every weekend. If you were to make $500 every weekend for an entire year just flipping My Little Ponies or going to the sale's section at Nordstrom Rack and putting the pants you buy on Amazon at full price, you could make $500 per weekend—super easy. That's an extra $26,000 a year. If you currently make $75,000 a year at your job, selling those small items to make a few extra dollars on the weekend takes you into the six-figure threshold. Using this logic, you can see that it's not hard to make money these days.

The lie that most of us believe about money is that it's hard to earn. That's because it was hard for our parents and grandparents. Of course it was. They didn't have social media. They didn't have computers. They didn't have companies like Monsanto growing massive crops with uniquely cloned seeds. They had to go out, plant their own stuff, and harvest it. They had to grow their own gardens and build their own houses. We don't have to do those things. Nobody is going to college right now to learn how to become an Instagram influencer (yet), although I personally know plenty of people who are making $10 million+ per year doing just that.

Jobs are different these days. You don't have to be a traditional mechanic or have a traditional desk job.

I agree with my friend Matt Manero—life begins at $100,000, and it gets good at a quarter-mil. Notice, we didn't say that you become rich at a quarter-mil. If you're making $150,000 right now and you need to level up, you have to get clear on what it takes to reach $250,000 per year so you can attain that goal.

If you're making a quarter-million, the next level for you is the half-million mark. Your focus needs to be on that. How much is that per day? How much per hour do you need to close? How many sales do you need to make per day and hour to hit that target? This is why, if you want to keep leveling up, you need precision and clarity, my friend.

If you're doing over half a million, congratulations! Your next step is a million. If you're in the millions, a whole new level comes along, as you can imagine. You'll start with one million, then 10 million, then 100 million, then a billion. The gaps get a lot bigger.

I'm not talking about money to sound like I have a callous heart and think money is all that matters. I'm talking about it because I want you to know what's possible. If a guy like me can do it, you have no excuses as to why you can't do it.

Next, we need to figure out what level we're on in business. To do this, we need to know where we're at. Are we an independent contractor or salesperson? Are we an employee? Whatever it is that we do for a living will determine our level. If you work for somebody else and are an employee, for example, you're on level one.

There's nothing wrong with that—there's nothing wrong

with being on any of these levels. Plenty of people make millions of dollars working for companies like Verizon, AT&T, and ExxonMobil. It's okay to work for somebody else, but when you want to level up in business, we have to be clear about what that means. Level one in the G Code Grind is being an employee or a salesperson. If you want to get to level two, you have to know the definition of level one.

Let's say that you want to level up from level one. To do this, you need to become self-employed because level two equates to a self-employed person. If you're a salesperson who wants to become self-employed, you need to know what steps to take so you can level up. This is what I mean when I talk about getting super clear about what you want.

If you want to get to the next level from working for someone else to working for yourself, you need to find financial backing for your business. This is your first step. Whether that means saving up your own money or relying on the bank, this step has to be taken so your business can stay afloat.

Second, you need to come up with an idea for your business. Third, you need to know the infrastructure. If you want to move up to level two, you must know what you have to do to be self-employed so you can become self-employed.

The difference between level one and level two is whether you're an employee or salesperson, but in both cases, your business revolves around you. This means that on level one, you collect a paycheck. On level two, when you become self-employed, it's all about you, too, because no one else matters in your world. You don't have any other people working with you, so you get to keep all the money—the same as if you were working for someone else. Level one and level two are the same in this way.

The next level is level three. This level goes beyond being self-employed. On level three, you're the CEO.

When you become a CEO and move up to level three, you have employees. You have teams. You have responsibilities you need to handle to run your business. Maybe you have office or warehouse space. Whatever your setup, you get paid last. You don't get to keep all the money for yourself like when you were working for someone else.

On level three, your mentality has to be that the company comes first. You're the CEO of a corporation. Your needs are on the back burner. I know that's contrary to how a lot of companies on Wall Street work these days, but that's how it works in our world. You're at the back of the line when you have a team and responsibilities to manage.

On level four, you become an investor and hire CEOs to run the companies you invest in. This is the pinnacle. It's not retirement; it's being able to sit back and let your money work for you. When you become an investor, you buy businesses. You buy real estate. You buy companies.

This is why you need to ask yourself right now where you're living life. Are you employed by somebody—level one? Are you self-employed—level two? Are you the CEO of a corporation—level three? Or are you an investor—level four? These are super simple questions that will quickly tell you what level you're on.

I'm between levels three and four as the CEO of two corporations and an investor in several different entities. We do everything from loans and software to real estate for business and franchises.

The point is, I know where I'm at. If I want to level up to be a full-time investor, I've got to level up my investments so that one day I can leave the corporate world and hire a replacement for myself. This is something I plan to do in the next five years.

Let's move on to Level 4 of the G Code: Group.

As we mature, we move into different levels of maturation. Level one, you're a child. Level two, you're an adult. Level three, you're a parent. Level four, you're a grandparent or great-grandparent. If we use these maturation levels as examples, we can observe that we were put here on Earth to evolve as human beings. We're born as children and eventually grow into adults, even though feeling like an actual adult comes at different ages for every one of us. Some of us feel like an adult at age 18 or 21. Some of us, like me, might be 35 before we finally feel like an adult.

The next level is to become a parent. You become responsible enough to bring more life into this world, which creates lineage. Then you become a grandparent, meaning the life that you brought into this world has brought more life into this world. That's the evolution.

Ask yourself what level you're on as a human being. Whatever level you're on comes with age and, in reality, having sex. But we still have to go through an evolution to progress through these levels.

Our relationships have different maturation levels, too, such as dating, being in love, being engaged, and getting married. Between dating, being in love, engaged, and married, that's four more levels.

Take some time to figure out which level you're on. Are you an adult? Are you a parent or a grandparent? If you don't have kids yet, and you want to level up in this area, then it's your duty to have or care for children.

I believe it's the duty of every one of us who is able and willing to make life. We are animals and conscious beings. That's what we're supposed to do: procreate and leave children to inherit the Earth. They'll probably do a damn better job of it than any of us have been doing because they'll have more information than we did.

I can't wait until the day that I'm a grandparent. I'm enjoying being a parent right now on level three with three young sons.

The day that I get to be a grandparent will be awesome. I'll get to send the baby home with the kids but enjoy all the good parts. That's the evolution. You get married, have kids, and then become a grandparent. When you level up in this way, you will experience amazing events in your life.

If you're married and don't have kids yet, the true test of marriage is children. So, when you say you want to level up your marriage and have kids, just know that the big boss at the end of that level is a motherfucker.

No matter the level you're on, it's likely you can go a level up.

Remember, for us to know what level we can get to next, we have to clarify where we are now in order to define our mission.

I hope I've helped you do this here in this chapter.

I hope I've simplified what you need to do, because as we go further into this book, you'll need to know your numbers. As the old saying goes, "What gets measured, gets improved."

In the coming pages, we're going to measure every area of our lives on levels from 1 to 4. This is simple to do. But the bigger meaning of doing this is that when you can start living a life of fours—meaning you will have a score of four on each level—you will truly reach greatness.

That's what the G Code is all about.

Since you're this far into the book, I know you're starting to dig in and understand the theme. As we go through each of these chapters, I'm going to keep drilling further so that what you're reading will make much more sense to you.

But before you continue on, I would love it if you would please hold up this book and take a picture, then share it on Instagram and tag me. If you're not on IG, share it on Facebook and tag me there. You can talk about what you've already learned and what you've applied to your life in the short period of time that you've been reading the *G Code*. Make sure to mention that your friends should read this book as well because it's a game-changer for everyone. It's a life-changer. We need to get it into the hands of as many people as possible. I greatly appreciate you being a part of this movement and helping more people reach their version of greatness.

By the way, you're going to love the next chapter.

7

THE SLAP

One of the problems that we face every day is the persistence of the force of average. This is the persistence of not being able to attain greatness. It's trying to distract us. This is what happens when the force of average slaps us in the face. I don't know about your life, but every single person I've ever met has one thing in common. We've all been slapped in the face by the force of average. Everything has been going great for us, and then bam, in a second, the distraction gets us, and we fall down and lose it all … or damn near all of it.

Do any of these examples ring true with you? You finally get a date with the person that you've dreamed of dating your entire life, only to show up late and not get a second chance. Better yet, you do date the person you've wanted to date your entire life, then you get drunk one night and sleep with his or her friend. Maybe you get into peak shape by dieting for 90 days, so you're absolutely ripped. Then you spend two years damaging your body, eating whatever the hell you want, and putting on weight. Or, you get your business running on all cylinders and then somebody important quits and customers get upset.

These are scenarios that take place when you're focused, but outside problems distract you. They slap you and knock you back down into what most people refer to as reality. We've all heard it: "Oh, he got knocked back down to reality." The truth is, you got knocked back down into the force of average. You got knocked back down to mediocrity.

If you don't want to get slapped anymore, keep reading. I'm going to rewire how you perceive the force of average's slap. If you choose to accept this rewiring that I'm giving you through this book, it will forever alter the way that you see problems, solutions, slaps, and everything in between. But once you choose to download this information, there's no going back without understanding that you've made the decision to regress and stay stuck in the way that you've always lived.

In moving forward with this new way of thinking that I'm about to download to you, know that you will have to make the choice to look at life in this new way or your life will never improve—your life will never get to the level that you want it to. Let me stress that you don't have to be in pain right now to want your life to be improved. You don't have to be in the shit storm to want improvement in your life. If you're not at rock bottom, looking to improve your life, the force of average has a choke-hold on you—no matter what you believe or hear, there's always another level up.

If we're going to rewire your mind, you have to accept that problems are tests. They're designed to hold you back from where you can go with a little work and focus.

Regarding tests, school teaches us backward. When we were in school, we learned a lesson and took a test. But in real life, we're tested, then we learn the lesson. Because of that backward teaching, we expect a test to come after what we've learned in life. This is why we get blindsided. School and real life don't match.

You get tested in your business and *then* gain experience from the lessons you learned from that test. You get tested in your marriage, *then* you become an experienced spouse because of the lessons you learned from the test. You get tested in your health, *then* you become more conscious and spiritually aware—that's the lesson.

Most people expect to take a test and get a reward. As kids, we were conditioned to getting a pat on the back for a good report card. While you might think this is funny, we've already discussed that between the ages of three and seven, how we feel, think, and perceive life shapes us. By the age of seven, we've already spent two to three years in school learning wrong expectations. We're wired wrong from the beginning; that's why it's important to get rewired right here, right now.

What we've learned and are used to is not entirely the truth. Tests do in fact come with rewards because lessons are rewards that lead to experience. We get experience from doing experiments, so if you want to become an expert, you've got to do the experiments in order to gain the experience to become an expert.

Instead of seeing tests as opportunities, most people encounter a problem and run. I know many people who've spent their whole lives running from problems, and they're still running. They're scared to face their demons.

Yes, life's a lot like that *Kung Fu* video game I talked about earlier, where you have to fight the big boss at the end. When I played *Kung Fu*, the big boss was bigger than all the other guys I had fought. If you were like me, you learned right quick that the big boss had a few extra moves you hadn't defended yourself against when the other guys were coming at you. He was strong and took a lot of hits. He really tested your skills. But once you beat the big boss, it unlocked the next level.

You might have thought you could take a breath after you beat the big boss, but when you got to the next level, it wasn't easier. More dudes kept coming at you, and a bigger boss loomed up at the end of that level. Then, as soon as you unlocked that level, more dudes came at you. This time, they dropped from the ceiling on ropes. After you kicked their asses, you got to meet the two big bosses at the end—twins.

This process continued all the way until you fought Mr. X at 10 levels deep. Mr. X was a bad motherfucker. If he beat you, you had to go back to level five and through all the same shit again just to work your way back up to him. When you finally beat him, you won the game. When you went back to play again, you could be any character.

Life's a lot like that video game. I didn't realize this as a kid, but I see it as an adult. Our problems are those guys coming at us horizontally across the screen. Our problems sometimes attack us two at a time. But we can handle them. It's a punch here, a kick there. We conquer these types of problems pretty easily. Then a few more problems level us, so once again, we punch, kick, sweep kick, and holler out, "Fuck you, problems." That keeps them at bay for a minute.

This tactic works until we get to the big boss at the end, when he represents a big problem. We can't fight him the way we've been beating back our smaller problems.

Now pay attention—I'm about to tell you how the big boss relates to you in your life.

If you want to level up and go to the next level, be it financially, physically, spiritually, emotionally, or with your network, you have to fight the big boss. That means you have a big problem.

It's one thing to have little problems, but life changes when you start changing what you want to do. If you want to do big things, you've got to solve big problems. That's just how it works on this planet. You'll never be in a position of greatness by just facing the smaller problems.

When most people get to the big problems in life, they turn around and run. In the video game, you couldn't do that. You couldn't back out of the screen once you'd moved further enough along to gain access to a new section of screen. You had to fight.

When I was incarcerated, my life was a lot like that game. I couldn't leave. I was behind walls, so I had to fight. But most people living a normal life on the outside refuse to fight. They can run away; they're not trapped. They have the option to refuse to solve the problem. Then their thinking gets all messed up. What they don't realize is that they don't actually have to fight the problem that's causing them so much pain—they just have to solve it.

To rewire your mind to level up, you need to start embracing your problems. You need to understand that problems represent an obstacle and give you a focus that you can use to beat the level. So every time a problem comes your way, celebrate. Instead of thinking like a victim, think about what the victory is going to be like once you beat it.

I want you to start getting ready for problems. I want you to start looking for them because when you do this, you can become a full-time problem solver.

It's not enough to make the proclamation, "I am now a problem solver." Make sure you're actually acting as a problem solver. I need to make this distinction because most people *say* they're a problem solver. Most people tell you that they *love* being a problem solver, but in reality, they run from problems. They fear problems. They stress over problems. Problems cause anxiety in their lives. They can't escape their problems. This might make them a "problem bitch" and a "problem sissy," but it definitely does not make them a problem solver.

You can't let problems control you and expect to move up

levels in your life. You have to embrace problems and understand that when you solve problems, you get rewards.

When you solve a problem with your health, you get a reward. This next story I'm going to tell you backs this up 100%.

I recently met a gentleman named Charlie Rocket, who once had a brain tumor. When he spoke on stage, I learned that he had signed 2 Chainz and several other music artists and was a huge name in the industry. When he was diagnosed with a brain tumor, he got out of the industry.

If you can believe this, he then did some research and figured out how to beat the tumor. Now this dude is a Nike athlete. Let me repeat that. Charlie beat a brain tumor and became a Nike athlete.

But how did Charlie do this? He got focused on solving his problem. When we get focused on solving problems, we get rewards. When we get really focused on our problems, just like Charlie, we can frickin' cure tumors.

That's how powerful focus is, but we don't use its power. We focus on the wrong shit. We don't focus on the problem. When we get slapped, we don't need to focus on the handprint on the side of our face and how it stings. We need to focus on the reason a person or the force of average was provoked enough to slap us in the first place. We have to solve the bigger problem, the root. It's not enough to focus on the problem itself; we want to focus on the solution.

When you embrace problems because you have an opportunity to solve them, and when you look for problems because you're a true problem solver, you get good at it. You're willing to do whatever it takes to solve problems, whether for yourself, the people around you, or the corporations that you run. Then, you get big rewards.

So many people run from their problems. They tell their therapists about them. They vent to their husband or wife about them. They vent to their coworkers. But not you. Not anymore.

You're solving your problems to get a reward—that reward is the next level.

But remember, there's always a bigger boss on the next level. And remember this, too: that bigger boss won't matter as long as you're practicing your problem-solving skills. You can be confident that no matter what comes your way, there's a solution. If you regard your problems with this mindset and refuse to be a victim, knowing that you will win at whatever comes at you, no one and nothing can stop you from leveling up. Nothing can keep you from getting everything that you desire on this planet, because you're focused on solving problems.

Let the rest of the world that's not living by the G Code be the victims of problems. Let them be taken down. We're focused on solving problems.

Bill Gates is a great example. The world needed computers. This was a problem. Bill made them happen. He then becomes the richest man in the world. Still, this wasn't enough for him. He starts to think something like, *The world has a problem. People are fucking sick and hungry. I'm going to help cure malaria and feed people.* Just like that, he donates $50 billion—his entire fortune—to resolve the problem. But this doesn't keep him down. He goes on to become the richest man in the world *again.* That's what you call solving problems.

I was just with Naveen Jain at a recent conference. Naveen is a billionaire. His company is creating something called preventative medicine, where you get an analysis of your body that tells you what you should and shouldn't eat, what you should and shouldn't do, and how your body is designed. It reads your genetics. When you get the results, you have a choice. You can do what the analysis says to do, or not. If it tells you that you can no longer eat cake, and you love cake, you have a choice to make. How much do you love cake versus how much do you want to feel better? When you follow the analysis results and don't eat the cake, amongst other things, you'll have a big payoff in 10 to 15 years.

The big payoff also occurs in other ways when you make good decisions across the key areas of your life.

You might experience good consequences when you solve the problem in your marriage. Why doesn't your wife trust you? Why doesn't your husband want to make love to you as often as you want it? Solve that problem. It's not your spouse's sex drive. We blame whatever the issue is on an outside source. But this is not the real reason. If you dig deeper, you might learn that they don't want to be with you because there are trust issues, for instance. Maybe you've belittled them. Whatever the problem is that's keeping you apart, solve it. Lift them back up and believe in them again.

I'm a firm believer in your spouse reading this book, too. They understand that there are problems in the marriage. When you guys beat those problems, you level up together. Your kids are going to have problems. When you come together as a husband and wife team, and you smash those problems, you level up together. That's why it's important that your spouse be in on this movement as well. Your marriage will improve, and every other aspect you share together, including parenting, will also improve.

Here's the big takeaway for this chapter: You are not a victim of problems. Problems are gifts. Problems are opportunities. People who solve problems achieve greatness.

Understand that problems come from the force of average, but your ability to beat problems is your ability to beat the force of average. Once you can beat the force of average by staying focused, you can beat the algorithm on this planet and become great. That's the formula. That's what I want you to use in your life from this day forward.

8

FORGIVE YOURSELF

If we're going to move forward and focus on a life of greatness, we've got to move away from the past that has anchored us to this mediocrity, this average, and sometimes even subpar existence.

So far, we've talked about the trials and tribulations that we've gone through. The force of average would have you believe that your situation is unique. And as you look around, you might think that everybody is keeping their secrets from you.

You might think that everyone else lives perfect lives and that your life is all messed up because of what you've done in your past that nobody knows about. Because of this, you think everyone around you is perfect, so you spend your whole life living with anxiety, resentment, regret, and other pent-up aggression inside you.

Allow me to share the secret that no one knows.

There's no perfect person walking on this planet. According to scripture, Jesus was the only one to ever do so without sin, and they killed him. So ask yourself, *Why in the hell do I want to pretend that I'm perfect?*

Nobody's perfect.

We all come from humble beginnings. Even if we lived an affluent lifestyle as a kid, the force of average has slapped all of us. I've never met a single person in my entire life who's not overcome or encountered a struggle. I've not met one person in my entire career who's coasted along to everything working out perfectly.

Let's be realistic and fair and recognize that some struggles are more powerful than others. If you were abused as a child versus running out of money as an adult, that struggle is different. Not all struggles are created equally.

I want you to work on thinking that the struggles that you went through, and the things that held you back, and any other trying instances that took place in the past, are not unique. They feel devastating to you, but at some point, and even right now, somewhere on the planet, someone's overcoming that same problem. You might think your problems are huge, but someone is alive right now who thinks they're small. When you think of life and your problems in this way, it puts everything in perspective.

You're going to think forward and not backward in this chapter. You're going to forgive yourself. By the time this chapter is over, you're going to reach a point where you will forgive yourself. When you can do this, you can move on and focus on being great.

We've already established that you get what you focus on. If you keep focusing on the struggles of the past and how you got to where you are now, but not on how you're going to get where you want to go, you'll continue to be in limbo. If you keep thinking in this way, you'll never break through that pattern.

Shit happens to all of us. Nobody's walking around with an ideal life. No one's life is clean.

You don't know what the people who fly private jets, drive Lamborghinis, and live what seems to be "living the dream" on social media go home to at the end of the night. You don't know what happened one second after a picture that looked Instagram-perfect was snapped. You certainly can't judge people according to what they put out on social media.

We have to focus on the fact that shit happens to everyone else *and* us. Then we've got to get past it.

Before you can get past what has happened, you have to forgive yourself. This is a similar process to what you would go through as a member of a program like Alcoholics Anonymous, Narcotics Anonymous, or any kind of addict program. The first thing you have to do is forgive yourself.

I'm a firm believer in forgiving yourself. If you don't take responsibility and get over it, you can't move on to what's next.

Think about having the perfect balance between being grateful for what you have while still being in pursuit of what you want. Before you can attract what you need, you have to forgive yourself so you can feel grateful for what you have. Believe it or not, what you want is all connected to this mindset.

Oftentimes, we think we don't deserve the good stuff that happens to us, even though we've worked for it. We earn money, then we end up spending it on hookers, blow, and all sorts of stupid shit because we don't feel like we deserve it—we haven't forgiven ourselves for our pasts yet. When we don't forgive ourselves, it breeds resentment. This leads to us feeling like we don't deserve what we've worked for, and we end up working hard to get rid of what we've acquired.

I've seen this time and time again in the thousands of people that I've mentored, coached, and consulted. I've seen the looks on people's faces from the stage when I've talked about this.

They relate to it, and it hurts to realize that they're punishing themselves over and over again.

In order to feel like you deserve what you're going to get and feel like you can achieve greatness, you have to forgive yourself. We can't go back and change the past. You and I don't own a time machine, and until Elon Musk gets his shit together and finally fucking creates one, we just have to forgive ourselves for what happened in the past so that we can feel like we have earned what we're going to get in the future.

You may *think* you've forgiven yourself. You might have tricked yourself into believing that, but subconsciously you still have forgiveness to unlock. The problem is that you don't know how to do this, but I'm going to walk you through how to do this right now.

If you're reading the book, go ahead and finish this chapter, then go back and do this exercise that I'm going to share with you. If you're listening to the book and in a car or office where you can't take a few minutes to close your eyes, then listen to this and come back to it later.

Whatever you need to do to complete this part, I encourage you to do it, because if you don't go through this exercise, you'll never truly get past what you haven't forgiven yourself for. I've paid tens of thousands of dollars to some of the best therapists in the world to figure out this code—this subconscious way of unlocking forgiveness inside ourselves. Now I'm about to walk you through it. Before you get started, I want you to understand the power of this exercise, but I also want you to be safe while you're going through it.

Assuming you're in a position where you can do this exercise without any distractions and without anybody around you, here's what I want you to do: Close your eyes and relax. It's okay to put your feet up on a desk or lie down on a couch or bed if you're at home. You can sit on a yoga mat or lean back on a weight bench. Wherever you're at right now, you can do this exercise to break through to the other side of self-forgiveness. It just takes a few minutes.

Now, with your eyes closed, think about the worst thing that you've ever done. Literally. What is the worst thing that you have ever done? It might be a betrayal, lie, theft, etc. It might be something violent. What it is doesn't matter. This is not the time for judgment. Just think about whatever it is as you're there in your comfortable position.

Feel the pain from that memory for a minute. Go all the way back and relive it, because this is going to be the last fucking time you do.

Next, remove yourself from the first-person point of view. Watch whatever it is that you're reliving as if you're looking at yourself. Maybe you stole a candy bar. Maybe you murdered a motherfucker. No matter what it is, I want you to think about the worst thing that you've ever done and go back and relive that moment from a third-person perspective.

You're seeing the worst thing play out as if you're the video camera recording the scene. You're not seeing it as if you're the actual person doing it. As you're watching this moment like a movie, look at all the surroundings. Look at all the circumstances that convinced you that you had to do what you did. What played out and led to that moment? What were all the thoughts that went through your mind?

Now here's the big question: If it wasn't you who did that thing, and you were a disinterested third party looking on, what would your judgment be?

You might answer that this person had to do what they had to do. If that's your response, then it stands to reason that *you* had to do what you had to do. When you have this realization, you know that there's no reason you should hold what you did against yourself.

When I looked back, I had to forgive myself. I was selling and doing drugs. I'm not proud of it, but I forgave myself for it.

Some people who do this exercise might reflect and say, "Man, I made a *series* of bad mistakes." Well, the fact that you're listening to or reading this book means that you want to move past it. It means that you're not the person you were back then. You are worth forgiving.

I'm not the person I was in the past, either. We grow more every day. I'm not the same person I was a year ago or even yesterday. Neither are you.

You have to understand that the naïve, misinformed person you were in the past lives in the past. You have to understand that who you are now is informed. You make better decisions. You've grown because of those decisions, and that worst experience was actually not something meant to hold you back. It was a stepping stone to propel you into your future. It was an experiment—an experience that you needed to leverage yourself to build your empire. You need to be thankful for that experience.

You need to be thankful for the worst thing that you've ever done in your life because, from this point on, that will be the lowest moment you've ever experienced. Maybe you're reading this book and haven't hit your low point. That's okay. You don't need to hit rock bottom to start to change your life. You can bounce back no matter where you are in life.

Be thankful for that low moment. When you anchor it to pain and suffering, you can use it to launch yourself into the greatness we're going to talk about. Doing this will absolutely change your life.

It's time to forgive yourself. What's done is done. Shit happens.

Forgiving ourselves is step one. Step two requires us to accept responsibility. When I did this exercise, I said, "I did it. It

92

happened. I forgive myself so that I can feel like I deserve what's coming my way." You can say the same thing to yourself.

Listen, if you don't get through this moment, experience, and exercise, and you don't let shit go, then wherever you're going in the future, you will have to carry this with you. Doesn't it seem like a good idea to let it go?

If you want the recommendation of a great therapist who will help you solve your problem—not just listen to you bitch—I recommend Dr. George Pratt in La Jolla, California. He also does digital training and works with high-level celebrities. I've personally worked with him, and so have many of my clients.

He's not inexpensive, but insurance should take care of some or all of your problems. Please only call his office if you're willing to do business. If you want to speak with him, $600 an hour will not only liberate you to become the best version of yourself but it might also catapult you to make $6 million a year or more.

Our third step is giving up control. You have to accept that you can't control what happened in the past. So you were abused, so your heart was broken, so you were incarcerated, so you screwed up financially, so you cheated, stole, and lied, so you caved into human tendencies and what the force of average uses against us every day to distract us. It happened. Accept it and ask yourself, *What's next?*

Next, you've got to decide to leave the past in the past. You've got to bury it. You can't bring it along with you.

Too many of us are trying to control things beyond our control. As I mentioned earlier in this chapter, you can't go back in time, so why try to control anything around it? Why try to control the story? Why try to control the narrative?

In other words, take control of your present, and take control of your future. The past is finished. There's not a single thing you and I can do to change it. We can apologize to people. We can pay people off if we owe them. We can try to make things right, but it's over; it's already happened.

The damage is done, so the best thing we can do is leave it where it already is—in the past. To move forward, we have to understand that if we're truly going to break free and get liberated, we have to give up control and realize that we can't change the past. The only thing that we're in control of is right now.

Here's the good news, if we're talking about something that happened years ago, you've already been punished for it—you've been beating yourself up about it for years.

Give up control.

Understand that the actions you take today affect you in the future. It's not what you did in the past that will affect you in the future; it's what you do today that's going to impact your future. That's exactly where I want you to get focused: on your future.

If you want to be great, you've got to get focused on your future. If you're going to strive to follow the G Code, it's about living in the now *and* in the future. It's not what you did in the past that makes a difference. It's not how cool you were in school. It's not how much money you used to have. It's not what companies you used to build. It's not who you used to bang. It's none of your old history. Where you're going and what you're doing right is part of the G Code.

Spend some time today forgiving yourself and giving up control. Declare your intentions out loud. Make eye contact with yourself in the mirror and say, "I give up control. I can no longer control the X, Y, and Z incident." If you're going to move forward, you need to do this. You need to announce that you're done punishing yourself and that you have no control over the past.

If you're going to move away from average and toward greatness, you've got to leave all the average and sub-average shit that you've done in your life in the past. Right where it belongs.

Only when you've done this should you move on to the next chapter, because this is the last chapter where we talk about the past. This is the last chapter of your life, and of this book, where you allow the past to haunt you.

In the next chapter and throughout the rest of the book, we're talking about the present and the future. I'm giving you a game plan to bring the visualization of the best version of yourself to life.

Please remember, if you don't go through all the steps up to this chapter, none of the stuff I'm about to give you about your future will matter.

Before you turn the page or continue listening, make sure you go through this process and forgive yourself.

Once you've cleared that obstacle, you can continue down the road to reach every dream you've ever imagined.

9

GETTING REAL

U p to this point, this book has been about your past. Now we're letting it go, rewiring your thoughts around it, changing your perspective, and learning from the experiences that you've had.

We've talked about your past because in order to move forward, into the present and the future, we have to let go of what has been holding us back in the past—while at the same time holding on to what will propel us into success in the future.

This is the pivotal part of this book, where we stop talking about everything that's led you to this point. In this part of the book, we're getting into the now. We're focusing on today and the future that has been written for us.

Understand, the actions that we take today will have direct consequences and effects 90 to 180 days from now.

The journey of the G Code that I'm about to share with you, and that you are starting right now, doesn't create change overnight. The change you want to experience won't even happen tomorrow or in the next couple of days. But in 90 to 180 days from now, you'll see the change. You'll feel the effects of what you're working on right now. Keep that knowledge close as you keep reading. Change is coming, but it won't be immediate.

The change that you want will come from living in the now, and that's what I'm going to teach you about—how to win every day in the only four areas of your life that matter. I'm going to share with you a routine that has gotten me through some of the darkest, hardest times that a human being could imagine.

Sure, some people out there have had it worse, but I assure you, my life has not been all rainbows and sunshine—as you've learned.

Despite the many times that I've gone to hell and back, I've kept the mindset that I'm about to share with you. Sometimes I didn't understand the mindset. It just took root in my head and I followed it, not knowing why I should, but I get it now. Since that time, I've broken that mindset down into an actionable plan that anyone can implement.

All it takes is sheer will, determination, perseverance, and consistency—then you will feel the effects of living a great life.

In terms of mindset, your life will take a turn for greatness immediately, and you will feel more positive. But again, for the real effects to kick in that will change your life, you'll have to wait 90 to 180 days. In addition to the good change that will makeover your life, you need to be aware of what's going to attack you when you hit 90 to 180 days—the force of average. You can't have one without the other, just like you can't have light without dark or good without evil. This is another law of the universe.

The force of average will try to stop you. It will say: "You don't need to follow the G Code anymore. Look how great your life is. *You* did this. You've improved enough, and you're a long way away from where you started. It's not the G Code that made all these changes. The G Code just happened to be moving alongside you. Let me distract you and keep you from following the code."

I guarantee that's what's going to happen to you when you hit 90 to 180 days. As soon as you start to feel the positive effects and all the benefits that you've been waiting for from choosing to live by the G Code, the force of average will barge in and distract you from focusing on the code. It will try to convince you that everything you've ever wanted that is now flowing into your life came about as a result of you doing it on your own, without following the code.

If you're wondering why I know this, it's because I've seen it happen thousands of times.

What I'm about to share with you is a simple routine. Anyone can take responsibility and make this routine happen. It doesn't cost you any money to follow through with what I'm about to teach you, but it will fight the force of average.

This routine doesn't hurt you physically. It doesn't hurt you financially. It doesn't hurt you spiritually. Instead, it will enhance your focus.

You can apply working out as an analogy of the routine I'm about to share with you. When you start in the gym and try to work out the first time, you're weak. Maybe you've worked out before but took a break for a couple of years before getting back at it. When you go back to the gym, and you're all weak, you might tell yourself, *Damn! I used to be strong.* The same applies when you're stepping into the G Code.

You're going to be weak in the beginning while you're learning the routine. It's going to be hard to focus because you haven't used your focus muscle for its intended purpose up to this point. Don't panic when you start working it out after finishing this chapter. I'm telling you that you're going to be weak. It's going to be frustrating. We also know that anytime we work on a weakness inside ourselves, it's frustrating in the beginning, so be prepared to ride that out.

That's another thing the force of average does. It frustrates you so that you don't enhance and strengthen your weaknesses. But you can't be a victim of that. You can't let the force of average get the best of you. You have to keep your head down and stay focused on the four areas of the G Code.

You already know the force of average is going to attack you, and its only means of attack is distraction. So if you're focused on the four parts of the G Code and don't give in to distraction or take your foot off the gas, you'll win.

Three to six months from now, you'll have wins so big, you'll look back in disbelief that you used to live the life you were living. You won't believe the life that you're living right now. That's a bold claim, but I've seen it happen. However, it will only happen if you stick to the G Code.

In this chapter, I'm going to teach you the G Code routine. In the following chapters, I'll break down why the routine is designed the way it is and why it matters to take the steps in a specific order.

Don't expect to get all the knowledge you need from this particular chapter. And don't stop reading after you figure out the routine. I already know what's going to occur—the same thing that takes place every time someone learns the routine—they think it's too simple and discredit it. That's the force of average at work again. It's going to tell you there's no way that such a simple formula will work for the complicated problems in your life.

This is a critical distinction that, once you understand it, will give you an edge.

Your problems are not complicated.

The way you think *about your problems is complicated.*

The truth is, problems are simple. They exist for everybody at every time on every frickin' imaginable universe and planet. Every living species faces problems. It's imperative to understand that every problem is solvable, and no problem is complex. It's how you handle, perceive, and even compound problems that make them complex. When this happens, the force of average begins to trick you. It says, "You're unique. Your situation's different. Nobody understands." But don't listen to it—remember it's saying these things to distract you.

This routine is going to blow your mind; it's so simple. But if you just stick to it, it will help you strengthen your focus muscle and excel in the only four areas of life that make a damn bit of difference.

Use this routine, and literally, you will live your dream life as you fight the force of average. It won't be an easy fight. The force of average will battle you for your attention every step of the way. That's why it's important to follow this routine—so you can defeat it.

Before you get started, use the app to put the daily routine right at your fingertips. It's absolutely free. Just go to GCode.-phonesites.com and follow the simple instructions. You'll record what you're doing in your daily routine, and it will keep score of how you're doing. Keeping score, and reviewing it every week, allows you to try to beat your best performance. Make sure you use the special cheat code GREATNESS that's 100% free when you download the app. But also make sure you don't give this promo code to anyone else. If people want it, tell them to get the book and get their own code.

Once the app is downloaded to your phone, the routine begins the next morning. The first thing that you'll do when you wake up is log into the G Code app. You'll start a new note and type in the five things you're grateful for.

Don't wait until you get to a laptop in the morning. Do it first thing, before you're even out of bed. We'll talk about why you need to use the app this way in subsequent chapters. But for now, just trust me on what to do.

After you've listed your five things, get up and drink a glass of water. Then, have a little protein to create energy in your body. After that, it's time to work on your genetics. You need to engage in some sort of exercise. Whether that means going for a run or bike ride, doing CrossFit, or going to Orangetheory or yoga, it doesn't matter. Just make sure that whatever you choose to do is challenging. Fuck waiting all day long to exercise—do it first thing in the morning. When you wake up, you're in peak shape. Science proves that the people who work out early in the morning are in their best shape of the day.[3]

Once you're done working out, take five minutes to meditate —just five minutes. If you have trouble meditating, buy a Muse headband from muse.com for $300-400. It will help you track your meditation. Or you can download the Calm app to your phone. I have the Muse headband and love it. Muse is a magnetic brainwave reader that tracks how you're meditating and tells you if you've done a good job or not. There's an app for it, too.

Next, we're going to address your diet. Let's say that, throughout the day, you typically eat a whole hamburger. If this is the case, reduce the amount of that burger you're eating. This routine doesn't mean you can't have a burger at all. But maybe you'll only eat three quarters and leave the last bite. If you're struggling to stay at a healthy weight, start cutting calories. That's part of your genetics, too. You want to be in great shape, so you need to start cutting calories. I'm not telling you to eat only what's on the Atkins diet, LA diet, or the cocaine diet. I'm advising you to just save a couple of bites. Eat a few less fries; maybe swap out a burger for a chicken sandwich or a turkey burger. You don't have to do anything dramatic. Just make a little change that you can stick to.

If we cut out a couple hundred calories every day, it adds up. A client of mine quit smoking in January, and in June, he made a post about how he had not smoked 5,500 cigarettes. That's an amazing number of cigarettes. Now imagine those cigarettes are calories. If you just cut out 10 or 20 calories a day, it adds up massively.

After you've worked on your genetics, it's time to go to work. Forget about trying to hit the traditional work-life balance. The balance that we're seeking is the balance between being grateful for where we are now and what we're in pursuit of next. In the meantime, while we're striving to hit that balance, we've got to show up focused at work.

When you get to work, you'll likely put in 8 to 10 hours. However, very shortly, I'm going to help you alleviate those hours. I'm going to show you how to get 48 hours' worth of work done in a 6- to 10-hour period—all because you'll have strengthened your focus muscle.

For now, you have to go to work. The kicker is that when you're done with work, you're done. Then it's time to focus on the people in your life.

After work, you're going to spend time with your significant other. If you're single, go on a date at least once a week. Whether it's with a chick or dude who's put you in the friend zone or you want to date someone of the same sex or the opposite sex, you're going on a date. It doesn't even have to be called a date. It could be a meeting. "Hey man, you want to meet at the bar?" Whatever you want to do in this area of the code, just plan on going out once a week, at a minimum, with somebody. The goal is to have an in-person, face-to-face meeting with another human being. Step out of your comfort zone. Try Tinder or Bumble if you need to, but make sure you're getting out. Remember, you've got to have this social outing once a week.

If you're a family person and have kids and a significant

other who live with you, when you get home, shut work off. Unless you're a police officer, firefighter, engineer, or heart surgeon, there are no emergencies. Nothing is going to change overnight that you could fix or that you need to remedy immediately. There's no reason to bring work home. Period.

Enjoy time with your family. Enjoy time with your friends. The goal is to make a point to spend time with another human being daily. And, remember, once a week, at a minimum, go out and have one-on-one time with somebody.

Once you have completed your goals for the day, you're done until right before bed.

At the end of the night, open up the G Code app and fill in your wins for the day.

These are the wins that you need to answer before you call it a night, as taken directly from the G Code app:

What are 5 things you're grateful for?

Did you work out?

Did you stick to your diet?

Did you have any wins today?

(Did you write down the five things you're grateful for? That's a win, btw.)

Who did you focus your time on today?

What is the lesson you learned today?

With the lesson, you can jot down a sentence, a couple of words, a paragraph, or several paragraphs. The length of what you write doesn't matter. Just record what you learned.

This should be the last thing you do before you go to sleep. When you're done, put your phone on your nightstand, knowing you'll start all over again tomorrow.

To recap, the G Code routine works because when we're forced to wake up and search our memory banks for things to be grateful for, we become a different human being. Most people wake up grumpy, but we're not having any of that anymore.

We're starting a grateful mindset fresh in the morning. When we do that, it gives us an edge.

We get a bigger edge when we work on our genetics. Most people are diseased because they don't work on their genetics every single day. That's not going to be you.

As it applies to focusing on our work, most people don't know what to do, especially entrepreneurs and salespeople. They get confused because they don't have managers or account-ability buddies. As the CEO, you've got to focus on the G Code.

Lastly, human beings are made to be a part of a network of other human beings. This is why it's vital that you spend time with your family, friends, and even just other members of society.

When you get plugged in and start tracking where you are in these four areas of your life every day, it changes your life. It changes the way your mind works. It rewires who you are from day one, so you become a different and better person—you become the person you are striving to be. Keep track of what's going on in your life, and in 100, 200, and 500 days from now, your life won't be the same. It won't resemble your life today in any way. My life's not the same, because once I started, I never stopped living the G Code.

The G Code will alter the future for you. It will allow you to bend the universe to your whim. This is real law of attraction shit, and it might be hard to accept, but the team and I live it. When we focus on these four areas every single day, I call it the law of action.

We're going to get into far more detail in each of these four areas as we move further into the book.

There's no excuse for you not to live this G Code. Give me 90 to 180 days of your life, and it will be changed—all through this simple process.

If you don't move forward and read more of this book, but

you do what I just taught you to do daily, in the order I shared, without wondering why, and without challenging the reasons behind the routine, your life will still be different. In less than six months, you'll feel like a different man or woman. Your mind will have discarded, unwound, and rewired decades of damage you've suffered through. Doesn't that sound like a really great reason to get started with the G Code today?

The G Code is the cheat code to greatness. Don't misunderstand; it's not a shortcut. To get to greatness, all it takes is for you to implement this code.

In the upcoming chapters, I'm going to break down the exact science behind why the G Code is as powerful as it is. You're going to love it. It's going to change your life.

I'm excited for you to experience the same miraculous changes in your life that I've been living in my life for years.

This brings us to a pivotal moment. You have a decision to make. You've been given the information. Now it's time to decide if you want to continue to be a victim of the force of average and fall back into mediocrity or you want to strengthen your focus muscle to get you literally anything you want on this planet.

Of course, you're going to keep reading.

10

THE FIRST G

G1: GRATITUDE

N ow you know the entire G Code process.

Moving forward, we're going to track how you're doing, but you need to sign up for a free account at gcode.-phonesites.com first.

This is not a traditional app, so you don't have to download any software. You don't even have to put anything on your phone. Just save the bookmark to your screen. If you don't know how to do that, you can find the instructions in our FB group, where there are all sorts of tutorials.

When you use the tracking app, it holds you accountable and becomes your personal daily journal.

The biggest thing to remember as you embark on recording your wins and lessons is that it all starts with gratitude.

Gratitude is the most important part of starting our day. This is why the first action that we have to take when we live the G Code is stating at least five things that we're grateful for. We have to write them down and see them; when we do this, we're programming our subconscious. But, we'll get into that later on in this chapter.

We want to tap into our gratitude first thing in the morning because our day hasn't started yet. We've just woken up and haven't had our coffee yet. We haven't had our Monster or Red Bull. Maybe our kids are screaming. Maybe a diaper needs changing, the phone's ringing off the hook, someone's pounding at the door. Whatever is begging for our attention might trigger us and make us a little upset. It might cause morning grumpiness.

Then guess what happens?

We might say something shitty or pull an asshole move. We might end up pissing somebody off because we started our day wrong. Once that happens, that crappy feeling spirals out of control for the rest of the day. You've been there. I've been there. We both don't want to go there again.

The solution is to start your day off thinking about what you're grateful for immediately—the second you wake up. This is your moment to be still before your day starts, before shit happens that irritates you. Plenty of things are going to distract you and trigger you into a bad mood; they'll make you crabby, and that will ripple out and affect other people.

We're going to start the day by combating that negative potential by using the G Code. The G Code gives you something to focus on so you can fight the force of average. All those distractions that trigger you in the morning weaken your fight against the force of average. Remember, the force of average, whether you want to believe it or not, is at war with you every single day.

Because of this, you have to prepare yourself for war. You don't want to be complacent. When you're grateful for what's in your life and where you're at in life right now, the force of average can't distract you with the bullshit.

First thing, when you wake up, immediately search your subconscious for five things to be grateful for.

Some people will rattle off a list in 30 seconds. Some will take two or three minutes. Some might struggle to find five.

My list varies like everyone else's. Some mornings I'm grateful for my bed. Some mornings I'm grateful for my pillows. Some mornings I'm grateful for my kids. Some mornings I'm grateful to be home. But every day, as soon as I wake up, I have programmed a habitual routine in my life to immediately think and write down five things that I'm grateful for as a part of the G Code. I do this religiously.

The second I wake up, I grab my phone, open up the Daily G Code app, and write down five things that I'm grateful for.

The most important part of your day is the morning when your hormone levels are reset after being depleted throughout the day. If you're a man, your testosterone levels are higher in the morning. If you're a woman, your estrogen levels are higher. We're programmed to be a beast first thing in the morning.

We wake up, recharge, and re-energize. But sometimes the beast comes out of us in the wrong way. We might check our email and see that somebody is late to work. Or we might get a text message and learn somebody canceled a breakfast appointment. Those things trigger us—and not in the right way.

When we get that text, we start talking about how they never show up on time and how they're disrespecting us. But when we start our day off with gratitude, when we start our day off searching our memory banks for things to be thankful for, right there in that moment, it activates our mindset differently.

Begin stimulating that thought process over the course of 21 days to create a habit, and you'll start waking up grateful in the morning. You'll wake up with no issues that will fuck your morning up. You'll wake up happy for where you are, what you have, and how you live while still in the pursuit of what's next—because greatness isn't a state of now; greatness is a state of next.

Here's why all this matters. The force of average attacks you when you're least able to defend yourself. When you wake up in the morning, you're foggy. Your brain's not running on all its cylinders. It's not pumping all the blood. Your sinuses are messed up. You're not dressed normally or at your peak performance. When you're vulnerable, it's an optimal time for the force of average to sneak in and distract you.

The force of average knows you're weak. But when you're focused on the G Code and the first thing you think about is what you're grateful for, you gain a head start on your day and start on the right foot; you've programmed your attitude against grumpiness.

Now let's be honest. We've all heard that money can't buy happiness, that there are plenty of rich and miserable people in the world, and that just because a person has money doesn't mean they're happy. This mindset is related to how people aren't able to find gratitude for where they are right now.

People say these things because they haven't been grateful, and they're not going to be grateful unless they make a big change. I want you to start this positive habit right this minute. It's pretty frickin' amazing.

When you program your subconscious to look for reasons to celebrate and appreciate, you train your brain differently. The brain is like a muscle. Let me give you an analogy to drive the point home.

A certain kind of curl that you can do with your fist is called a hammer curl. If you only do hammer curls, your bicep will grow a certain way. But, if you do hammer curls plus preacher curls, your bicep will look different than if you were just doing hammer curls. Start doing hammer curls, preacher curls, plus a variation of barbell curls, and your biceps will take shape differently than if you only did the first two exercises separately or together.

Let's say that all your life, your biceps have been one way.

But at the age of 45, instead of just doing hammer curls, you decide to do preacher curls. It might take a while, but doing this will literally change the shape of your muscles. When you change up this exercise, you'll redesign the grooves the muscle tissue cuts underneath your skin.

Now think about this ...

The same thing happens in the brain. It, too, is a muscle. When we take away the negative distractions from the force of average and add in gratitude and a positive exercise that builds up a different part of the brain, it reshapes the way our minds think. We start looking for things to be grateful for instead of things to be pissed off at. Isn't that a great way to fucking live life?

Imagine going through life and getting cut off in traffic, but you're just grateful the other driver didn't hit you. Imagine going through life and losing a job, but you're just grateful to be where you're at while looking forward to the next opportunity. Imagine going through life and losing the person you thought you loved, then you realize there's love everywhere because you have an abundant mindset.

Imagine that instead of looking for a reason to be depressed and angry, and fucking ruining your life, you rewire your brain to find reasons to celebrate, appreciate, and stay alive. What you're doing becomes habitual, and that's the best benefit.

America has had more mass shootings in 2019 than there are days in the year. We have a mental health issue. We can argue about guns and everything else, but if you're mentally unhealthy, you'll do things that you normally wouldn't do. You'll do things that sane people like you and I can't understand.

While this epidemic of shootings might be a little extreme to use as an example, we have to start working not only on our mental health but also on our subconscious health. We've got to start working on what we hear. We've got to start working on what we're grateful for. We've got to start rewiring our brains because that's where the force of average has gained a grip.

The force of average knows that your amygdala—the part of your brain that triggers the fight or flight mechanism—still needs stimulation. It doesn't matter that we're not running around worried about being chased by lions and saber-tooth tigers; our brain doesn't know the difference between various modern stressors and a beast hunting us down. It kicks into gear to protect us even when we don't need it.

We worry about what somebody says on the internet or about what piece of paper was signed by a government entity. The truth is, our amygdala needs to be stimulated. The force of average knows this, so it uses the media, gossip, magazines, publications, videos, social media, and every other bombarding method it can to ignite fear and anger. When we're angry or scared, we're distracted. But when we're grateful, we're focused.

As I've said time and time again throughout this book, focus is everything. When human beings are focused, we go to the moon. We go to Mars. We redraw maps. We change the way energy works in this world. We upset markets. We change countries. It's insane what we can do when we get focused. The force of average knows this. That's why I'm telling you about what works—that's why I'm telling you that the first way to get focused is to be grateful for what you have so that you can focus on what's next.

We have a mental health epidemic right now where nobody's grateful for what they have. Somebody's better than you on social media. Somebody's better than you in the gym. Somebody looks better and feels better; they're faster or slower. They have more likes and more followers. They're better at video games and sports than you.

We have to accept that there's always going to be somebody

better, but that it doesn't matter. Most of us are really competitive and negative, but hear me out. We chase after what everyone else has and compare ourselves to others instead of just being grateful for who we are and what we have. The freedom of feeling better than okay is in our mindsets, and when you tap into the right mentality, you won't care what anyone else is doing. You'll be too grateful to notice.

It's not a pill that we need. It's not more medicine that we need. It's not more drugs or alcohol that we need.

We need gratitude in our lives.

When you're grateful for who you are, people catch that vibe. They want to love you. People want to be with people who are like that.

Danny Galvez has worked for me in my office for about two years now.

There's just something about him. He's grateful to be alive. This dude wakes up with a smile and lives his life by the G Code every day. Everybody loves Danny because they can tell he's grateful to be where he's at. He's grateful to be alive. He knows he's on the path, making big moves. And he's grateful as fuck.

People want to be around that type of person. People want to catch that person's energy. You start working on subconscious mental health by being grateful. When you adopt this mindset, people become grateful for you. Think of how many people you can introduce this process to and how many people you can share dailygcode.com with. Think of how many people you can share this book with and how that will help them. Think of what you can do to inspire people.

If you live your life in this way and share the G Code with as many people as you can, imagine how many people will have your name on their gratitude list every morning. That's the real win right there. That's how you feel loved. That's how you work on your mental health. It's not another pill. It's not repression. It's simple.

Be grateful for what you have now. Other people will be grateful for you when you're grateful for them, and that's the first step to the G Code: Gratitude. It's time to reprogram your brain. You've been angry. You've been mad. You've been unhappy. You've been dissatisfied. You've been upset. And you've been anxious long enough.

It's time that you become grateful. Generate gratitude in your life, and in doing so, you'll become loved by those around you, just as you love yourself.

The first step of the G Code is being grateful. Every other positive moment in your life that follows today stems from gratitude. And that means everything you have ever wanted in your life stems from gratitude too. This is the first step to take toward attracting what you want and need.

11

THE SECOND G

G2: GENETICS

I've been on a very strict exercise routine since I was 19 years old. When I found out I was going to be incarcerated for a couple of years, I wanted to make sure that I got into shape. I knew I needed to kick my physique up a notch to survive on the inside.

Until then, I'd never paid much attention to or cared about my fitness. I was always the skinny kid. A lot of folks look at me these days and say I'm in good shape for a 40-year-old. I have big arms and have built up my muscles. But for years, I still thought of myself as that skinny kid. For years, I worked out in the same way and in the same gyms where I worked out when I was a kid.

But we evolve as human beings in every area of our lives, especially in our physicality, so things change. And they should. A lot of people devolve; we'll talk about that in this chapter.

As we evolve, we have to adapt and change. I got into a pattern that I think may resonate with you. I would continue to do legs on leg day, chest on chest day, arms on arm day, and so on. My routine was to do 5 sets of 10, then rotate to the next thing. I had been doing the same shit forever. But once I crossed the 35-year-old mark in my life, my genetics slowed down. I developed a little gut, and asshole people on YouTube pointed out that I had man boobs and was getting out of shape.

I thought, *Damn, I'm still working out. I'm still going to the gym three to five times a week.*

I was still doing the same stuff that used to work for me when I was in my 20s. But I was getting older, and my metabolism was slowing down.

When most people find it gets harder to do something, they let it go. But exercise is the longest commitment of my entire life. I have been in an exercise routine for 21 years now.

Still, it's gotten harder as I've gotten older. It's not as easy to spring out of bed in the morning. My back hurts more than it used to. My muscles ache a little bit longer.

When I noticed this change, I started digging into biohacking secrets and had the pleasure of meeting Dave Asprey, who was speaking at an event. When I spoke with him, he gave me a bunch of information that I was able to use. I knew that if I'm going to keep pushing through life, if I'm going to be worth hundreds of millions of dollars, or be a billionaire, if I'm going to change lives, if I'm going to fill up stadiums and accomplish everything that I've been led to and called to do, I have to keep up with my health.

Another turning point in how I viewed my physical fitness happened when I had a conversation with the guy who had been the CEO of a prominent company for 37 years. When he retired, he decided that since he'd gone to the gym every day, he could let his health go. He's now about 80 years old, and during our conversation, he said, "Ryan, the biggest regret I have in my life is that I stopped exercising. I'm 80 years old. It's too late to get in the game now, but I saw a guy on TV who never quit. He didn't look a day over 60."

Your body is a reflection of how you feel about yourself. If you're going to have great things in your life, you have to keep working it, just as you work all of the other three areas of the G Code.

If you've let your body go, I know you're unhappy walking around and looking that way. I'm not saying that from a vain place. I'm saying that if you're overweight, just like I've been, and like many people are right now, you're not happy about it. I don't think being overweight is a disease, either. It's not something that's out of your control. Now, I do highly recommend getting tested to figure out what food allergies and sensitivities you may have that might be contributing to your weight gain, but for most people, getting your weight under control simply calls for a few changes in your genetics.

When you get focused on these changes and follow the same exact process daily, it'll help you beat what you're dealing with.

Now, you might be thinking, *He's full of shit. I'm not even going to finish reading this book. I love me, no matter what.* I ask you to bear with me. What you're reading is tough to hear, but I'm saying everything out of love. Try to lay down your defenses and hear my message to you.

If you're thinking, *I do love myself. I might be a little out of shape, but I do love myself,* imagine how much more you'll love yourself when you're stronger, healthier, and more beautiful in the eyes of other people.

We know that people who look better, feel better. They have higher confidence. They secure jobs, raises, and bonuses more easily. If two people—one better looking and one average looking—have the same skills and compete in a sales pitch, the better-looking person's going to win, even though they both have the same set of skills. Not choosing the ugly motherfucker is natural selection. This is the evolution that so many of us try to fight.

The media tries to hype up fat-shaming, saying how wrong it is. They try to normalize being overweight—as if it's good for you. The truth is, you owe it to yourself to be fit. You owe it to your kids. You owe it to your employees and your legacy. After reaching the ages of 50 to 60 years old, a lot of people retire. They haven't taken care of themselves and when they fly, they can't fit in the seats! When they go on vacation, they eat up all the fatty meals and snacks, then they wonder why they feel like shit the other 11 months of the year. I'm not telling you this to knock you. I'm telling you this because I want you to be healthy and stick around for a long while.

You have to focus daily on your genetics. If I've been working on my genetics since I was 19 years old, you can start working on yours now.

You're going to have to level up. If we're going to focus on being great—as in getting in great shape—this is what we're going to have to do. Being great requires that you're great on all levels. Your greatness and ascension into the best version of yourself requires your physical greatness; it requires your best stamina.

You've got to get control of your diet. My trainer, Marc Zalmanoff, told me when we started working together, "You don't have to follow a fancy diet and go all Atkins, keto, or anything else. Those are fine options if that's what you want to do, but here's what I propose that's easier and still effective. Instead of eating a whole hamburger, eat a half or maybe three quarters. Instead of eating a handful of fries, eat two or three. If you're still hungry 20 or 30 minutes later, eat again. But chances are you won't be." That's why I follow his advice of moderation that I laid out earlier. It works. I love it because it's easy to remember, too. Just eat a little less. I know you can do that!

Next time you're hungry and find yourself walking into the pantry, ask yourself, are you eating out of boredom, or is your body craving nutrition? Ask yourself the next time you open the cupboard and are about to grab a bag of chips if a banana would work instead. Little tweaks make all the difference in the world. As a guy who's 40 years old and at 12% body fat, I don't have a special diet. I love me some Mexican food and tacos, but instead of eating six tacos, I might eat two.

We come from a time where Momma made us clean our plates—especially those of you around my age. So that's what we think we're supposed to do. We think restaurants charge us insane amounts of money for a chicken-fried steak, then the server brings this huge steak, and because Momma told us to clean the plate, we shovel down the whole thing.

Add overeating to not exercising, and the calories stack up. We get slow and lazy and caught in a spiral, making it easy for the force of average to put a chokehold on our genetics.

That's when you start having surgeries and living a life on medicines. I'm 40 years old and take no prescription meds. I go to the doctor and hear, "How the hell are you even this healthy?" I'm telling you, I'm not doing anything special other than focusing on my genetics.

You can't say that I'm gifted genetically either. Look at every other male in my family and you'll see that I have to put in the work. I'm focused on being great; that's what the G Code is about, and diet is a huge part of it.

You know that another part of your genetics is exercising. You have to have rigorous exercise in your life, especially if you're over the age of 35. As you get older, you need to work out harder than you've ever worked out before because the force of average is coming for your old ass. You have to push. Don't be the retired CEO who said, "The biggest mistake that I made was not continuing to work out. Now it's too late."

Find somebody who will hold you accountable. I have a personal trainer, and when I show up at his place four days a week, he tortures me for an hour. I hate it while I'm going through it, but I love it when I'm done. And I love the results. So does my wife. So does my audience. My kids love it when I make this investment into my genetics because I have the stamina to go four-wheeling with them.

It wasn't long ago that while I had one kid strapped to me in a badass military-looking baby carrier, another kid got stuck in quicksand. At 40 years old, I was strong enough to pull the kid out of the quicksand with another kid attached to me. That emergency situation wouldn't have gone down the way it had if I didn't have somebody holding me accountable to a daily exercise regimen.

You might think, *Well, hiring a personal trainer is a lot of money. I can't swing that.* I'm going to argue with you here: a personal trainer costs a few hundred dollars a month. Imagine what diabetes medicine costs. Imagine what heart medicine costs. Imagine what heart *surgery* costs. Imagine what cholesterol pills cost every month. Hell, I'd rather give the money to Marc than big pharma, but that's just me.

Another huge part of your genetics is that you have to get some sun. A lot of you are walking around pasty, itchy, dusty, and ashy—but I want to tell you, the sun's good for you. A lot of folks these days lurk in social media and get sun through the window. We live inside offices, cars, hotel rooms, and apartments, but that's no excuse. You have to get out and take in some sun. You've got to get outside in nature.

Recently my wife and I traveled to Coeur d'Alene, Idaho, and right outside the balcony of our hotel was a decent sized mountain. I'm from Texas, so anything bigger than 10 feet is a mountain to me. We decided to head over to that mountain. We wanted to be outside and soak up the mountain, soak up the sun, breathe in the air, and sweat a little. We could have easily ordered room service and fattened up, but we didn't.

You have to get outside. You have to get some sun. One of my favorite exercises is surfing. I'm horrible at it, just like I'm horrible at golf, but I love it, because being in the ocean or any other body of water is the only time you can truly submerge yourself in mother nature. You can't do that in the mud. You can't do that in the sand. It doesn't feel good. But there's something about getting in the water. So, in your everyday health regimen, include the water, sun, diet, and exercise. They matter, and you need to focus on them every single day.

Finally, when it comes to talking about genetics, we have to include love. Being loved gives your genetics a boost. You have to be loved. And to be loved, you have to give love. When a human being feels the connection and love from another human being, there's something magical about it. It makes us feel better.

We've all seen or heard of little kids in the hospital who get a visit from their favorite hero who tells them that they love them. The kid starts feeling better, gets out of bed, and starts walking around. As human beings, we need that kind of love. And we know that, at their lowest, these kids that hear what their heroes have to say to them are feeling it. They're fueled by it.

So don't forget about love when it comes to focusing on your genetics, and don't minimize its power.

Don't forget that we need our diet to be correct and balanced and that we need to turn away larger portions.

Don't forget to engage in great exercise. It needs to be rigorous enough that it forces us into the pain of growth—especially if you're over 35.

Don't forget that we've got to be outside. We're wired into this planet, so we need to spend some time outdoors rooted in nature—in the essence of where we come from.

This is my morning ritual:

Every morning, without an alarm, I wake up between 5:00 and 6:00 AM. I immediately open up my Daily G Code app on my phone and follow the process that I mentioned earlier and will get more into later on. After I'm done recording what I'm grateful for, I drink some water and grab a Red Bull or Monster. (I know it's bad for me, but I do it anyway. I'm a human being; I have a few vices.) Then I head to the gym.

At the gym, I write my Facebook posts while sitting in my truck in the parking lot. Then I put my phone down, and for the next hour, I'm Marc's bitch. Whatever Marc tells me to do, whether I like it or not, I am his slave. When we're done, I head back to the house and have a 1st Phorm Level-1 Bar. I don't get paid to promote them, but the owner of the company, Andy Frisella, is a friend of mine. I've tried a million protein bars, and the Level-1 Bar is the best and most delicious. I even take them with me when I travel. After my protein bar, I go to work for the day.

You want to get your genetics and exercise in early. Your body needs air, water, and food. That's why I drink some water before I have my Red Bull, and that's why I exercise first thing in the morning. It sucks to wake up early and exercise, so I'm going to do the two things that suck the earliest so I can get on with what's more pleasant. As my friend David Goggins says, "If it ain't hard, we don't do it." But that's a whole other beast mindset.

If I get the hard stuff out of the way early, I don't have to spend the whole day worrying about whether or not I have to go to the gym. I'm focused and locked in from the moment I wake up.

Since I mentioned 1st Phorm, I want to tell you that they have a program called 75HARD. It's a very, very rigorous diet and exercise routine that you go through for 75 days. I've personally seen hundreds of my friends and associates come out of it a changed person. If you're looking for something to push you, give it a shot. It's not easy. It's hard. That's why they call it

75HARD. You need to look into this program if you're searching for a regimen that will challenge you. It's also absolutely free.

I want you to think about exercise in the long term. My friend, Mike Hearn, has been on more fitness magazine covers than anybody else in the world. He's 50 years old; a Mr. Universe married to a Mrs. Universe, a gentleman, and a great guy. Mike used to be on *American Gladiators*. I was working out with him at Gold's Gym—the old mecca in Los Angeles—a few weeks ago when he came up to me and said, "Stewman, are you still lifting heavy?"

I said, "I just do squats in the 300s, sometimes deadlifts in the 400s, but on a regular, I'm lifting 285 to 315 on my sets of squats, ass to the ground."

He said, "Stay lifting heavy like that because as you get older, your bones start to loosen up. They get softer. It's called osteoporosis. But if you continue to lift heavy, when you're older, your bones will stay denser, and you'll end up stronger. You won't break a hip. You won't be prone to a fracture, strain, or bone spurs because you will have kept your bones dense from applying the pressure." That's a big metaphor for life right there—keep applying the pressure to be stronger.

Thriving under pressure keeps you dense. It keeps your skin tough so you can go through the hardships of life.

Even as I share that story, the force of average wants to tell me, "Oh, you've been lifting long enough, take a break." So be ready to hear the same thing—the force of average telling you that you don't have to exercise today. You made money, after all. The force of average will try to trick you into bad ideas that will eventually hurt you, making suggestions like, *Just pick up this light weight.*

But if one of the most elite bodybuilding people in the world says that you have to continue to put massive amounts of pressure on your bones and lift right, so those bones can continue to stay dense and you can fight osteoporosis, I'm all in. And I hope you are, too.

When you get older, you're not supposed to make things easier on your genetics. When you get older, things are actually going to be harder because you've got a lot more to lose. Combine that with the force of average trying all the old and new tricks on you to grab your attention, and that means you have to push even harder.

Listen, if you don't follow the path to greatness in your genetics, the rest of this shit's not going to matter anyway.

Nothing would be worse than if you had all the money and love in the world but you chose not to exercise and diet properly. You'd find yourself stuck in a hospital bed while your family does what you love to do without you. Every other influential and Instagram person on the planet will pass you by—all because you decided not to take care of yourself. Maybe you're in a wheelchair because you lost a foot. Well, you still need to go hard on your genetics. This is real stuff. It may seem far off to you, but if you don't prepare yourself today, what good is all that money going to do if you can't spend it with your family? What good is all that love people want to give you if you're not there to get those hugs on those family vacations because you can't travel?

When it comes to the G Code, working on your genetics is part of the quest. There's a reason genetics is the second G in the G Code. There's a reason the routine starts with waking up, noting the five things you're grateful for, and then moving into your genetics. Genetics are important. I want you to live long and prosper. But if you're going to do that, you have to make sure you focus on your genetics daily: diet, exercise, sun, and love.

12

THE THIRD G

G3: GRIND

The third G in the G Code is grind. Now, what I call the grind is your job. When people say, "Man, I gotta go grind it out," or "I gotta get on my grind," they mean they have to get to work. A lot of us enjoy our jobs, but that's not the case for everybody. The key is to make the most of your job and be efficient with your time. The ongoing theme of this book, message, and lifestyle is focus. Focus on the right things. Focus on your grateful mindset. Focus on your genetics. Focus on the grind that pays your bills.

Some of us are entrepreneurs, and we love what we do. Some of us are entrepreneurs, and we hate what we do. You don't have to be a business owner or manager. You don't have to be the boss. Regardless of what you do, we're going to focus on you being great—because you can be great regardless of what you do.

Before we get into the grind, I want to tell you a story.

When I got out of prison in 2002, I got a job at a car wash. All I knew was that if I was the best car wash person on the planet, I had a shot at owning a car wash one day. It was not a guarantee, and it hadn't been talked about by management or anything like that, but I knew I had a shot. I had to be able to do everything if I wanted that car wash: knock it down, break it up, tear it apart, build it back up again, service it, shine it, wax it, trim it, Armor All it, everything. So, that's exactly what I did. I set out to be great at being in the car wash business. I was a young man at the time, and as I look back, I know I was focused on the mission to own that place.

The reason I share this with you is that, after about two years of hard work, dedication, and complete focus, something happened that changed my life.

A lady came into that car wash and offered me a job in a different industry. I took the job because I was glad the place had air conditioning. That's when I became a mortgage broker.

Somebody had recognized my greatness. Somebody had recognized my efforts. Somebody had recognized my hard work. I want you to hear about what happened to me because you might be out there working for somebody else right now, but barely getting by. If this is the case, you're not doing what it takes to be great in your business. You're not doing what it takes to be a great employee. You might be an employee, but you're not doing what it takes to be great. When you're working in your greatness, you'll do a lot more than just get by.

If you do the right thing long enough but the company that you work for doesn't notice, the companies that you service will. Or one of your customers will, like one of mine did.

I'm not bringing this up to push you to work as hard as you can in order to achieve self-satisfaction. The whole point of this book is to do the work and focus on the four areas I'm introducing you to, no matter what. This chapter is about the actual work portion, the grind.

I'm fortunate I love my job. I love the people I work with. I get to write books like this, make videos with positive messages, and talk to people on social media. That brings me a lot of joy.

Don't get me wrong; my job can be stressful just like anyone else's. When you've got half a million people following you on social media, you get about 500 DMs a day, and the way I'm built mentally makes me want to acknowledge them all. I hated it when I was on the come up and sent people DMs but nobody would acknowledge me. I don't want to be that guy who forgets where he came from. I want to be the Mouth of the South, the people's hero. But, it can be stressful because, as I'm trying to get back to everybody, I'm working in other jobs and flying around the world. I speak on stages and travel all the time now. It's a hectic job, but boy, I love it. At least, that's what I've convinced myself.

When you run as many companies and events as I do, and have as many clients, the only way to get to the level of greatness that I'm going to explain to you today is to be focused.

Most people in business say, "I want to be a millionaire." But they're not being specific. They're being vague. If they say, "I'm going to make millions of dollars," questions need to be answered. How many millions? What kind of millionaire do you want to be?

The force of average wants to keep your language vague so that your subconscious isn't clear about what the intentions and outcomes are that you desire. When we give ourselves a vague goal, our subconscious goes, *That's vague. We don't know what it is, so let's not even work toward it.* When you use vague language, you don't realize what's working against you in your mind.

The G Code is all about getting focused and moving toward your goals in micro amounts. We're going to focus minute by minute and hour by hour while we're in the saddle. We talked about waking up, meditating, and being grateful. Then we talked about taking care of your genetics. These are non-negotiables in your life. This isn't a code where you can pick and choose what you want to work on. You can't say, "I like everything but the working out part." Or, "I like everything, but I'm not businessy." Every part of this code is all or nothing. The G Code is the code to being great, not the code to being great in some areas and just okay in others.

We've established that you have to go to work. Work starts for me around 11:00 every day. That's when I dig in at the office. Truthfully, work starts the minute that I wake up because there are other things that I have to work on before I can actually make it to my office.

I run my entire life by a scheduler. Every single thing is on it. You want me on your podcast? Here's my scheduling link. You want me to do a video with you? Here's my scheduling link. We need to have a conference call? Here's my scheduling link. We have a meeting? Here's my scheduling link. Oh, we have to go somewhere? Here's my scheduling link—block a time on my calendar.

There's a reason that I manage my time this way. As entrepreneurs, business owners, and oftentimes even employees, we lack leadership. There's no boss, manager, or CEO. We're that person, as I mentioned.

When we're in charge of our time and accountability, we intend to be focused, and we think we're focused, but oftentimes, we're not. And if we're not focused, we're not tracking and measuring our goals. The reason I time block every single thing on my calendar while I'm at work is that it keeps me accountable to myself. If I see that I have 30 minutes to finish a task, I'm on the grind. I'm not fucking off. I'm not zoning out. I know I have 30 minutes to knock that task out, and that means I'm racing the clock. Attacking and completing my tasks like this is no different than doing CrossFit in the morning. It's a must-do, and it's non-negotiable.

The other reason I schedule everything is that, at the end of the day, I can look back at my calendar, see everything I did, and track my wins. Tracking your wins is part of the G Code, too. You'll learn more about how and why to do that in a couple of chapters.

Many people get a lot of stuff done, but others don't get anything done. You might feel like you accomplished nothing, but you don't realize how many items you checked off your to-do list because you don't track them. I could ask you right now, "What did you do at 2:30 today?" You might answer, "I don't know. About that time, I was behind my desk." If you asked me what I did at 2:30 today, I could tell you exactly where I was, who I spoke with, and how the conversation went. Why? Because I'm focused and I keep track of my day with a scheduler.

When I decided I wanted to make $1 million in a year, a few years back, $1 million seemed like a lot of money. Then I broke it down to $3,000 a day. Nowadays, $3,000 doesn't sound like a lot of money to earn to me, but it might to you. I set that goal and started attacking it daily. I kept my head down and focused—and by the time the team and I got to the end of the year, we'd almost doubled our goal of $1 million.

When you get focused on a monetary goal in business and boil down the plan of how much money you want to make a year, especially if you're in sales and entrepreneurship, you need to know what you have to do daily to make that happen. You need to ensure that you're setting time blocks every day to reach the steps you set out for yourself.

It's going to be a pain in the ass to write everything down in the calendar, and I realize I just put another step in the way of your goals, but I'm telling you, when you're laser-focused on your grind and you know exactly what you need to do every minute of the day, you'll experience the greatest byproduct of that. You also don't have to try to remember to do shit. When somebody tells you to do something, you don't have to remember it. Put it in the calendar and do what you need to do at the appropriate time.

You can't lose with this system of time blocking every single thing on your calendar. When you wake up in the morning, after you do your gratitude exercise, you can look at your calendar and see what you have to do for the day. There's no such thing as an emergency in business either. As we've discussed, our so-called emergencies aren't as big as we think.

In my office, people know I'm all about focus. They know that when I'm in the zone, I'm in the zone. I have a little door hanger outside my office that says, "Do not disturb. Recording in process." People know when that door's shut nobody is to go in there—not even if a client swings by. My team knows that when I have the door shut and the hanger on it, it's an important time for me. I am focused.

We have a saying around my office: "48/7." That means we can do 48 hours' worth of work seven days a week or two days' worth of work in one day. The reason we can do this is that we're laser-focused and live by a schedule. My sales guys live and die by a schedule. Our tech support team lives and dies by a schedule. Our managers live and die by a schedule. You might think that's hardcore, but when you schedule everything, you know what you're about to do. You can follow through with your plans, you're held accountable, and you get to track your wins.

If you're an employee, the same rule applies. You know what you have to do every day, so you can schedule it out. When you're laser-focused, you get more work done than you've ever done before, your boss is less likely to give you a hard time, and you're more likely to get raises and bonuses. You may even end up getting recruited by a another company or person who recognizes your efforts. Also, in the event that you ever need to back up your word, you've got the entire calendar of everything that you've done in front of you for months and months, or however long you've been in the routine. That's going to impress your superiors! I can tell you everywhere I've been and every job I've done for the last eight years because it's all in my Google Calendar.

Living the life we want is all about focus.

When most people are at work, they focus on what they don't like, the aspects that they don't enjoy. Or, they focus on the fact that they have to be in the office and aren't at the beach, on vacation, or hanging out with Instagram influencers in Mykonos. But when you stay focused minute by minute, hour by hour, day by day, all your anxiety and all your wishing and waiting go away. Eventually you build an empire; you stack money and take vacations, and you might even take some influencers along with you.

The takeaway is, if you're going to be great in business, you've got to stay focused.

As I told you before, when it comes to business, there are four levels you need to be aware of. We're going to talk even more about those levels in a later chapter. You'll even learn how to grade yourself in business and in all four areas of your life using specific numbers and measurements of the G Code.

For now, I want you to absorb the fact that business fuels everything. The money that I make in my office gets taken out into the marketplace. It puts my kids in private school. It offers them a way better life than I had. It often allows my wife and kids to come with me when I travel because I can pay for people to help with our home office. It allows me to create job opportunities for the amazing people who work for my companies.

A lot of people think, *Money is evil*, or, *I don't want more money*, blah, blah, blah, and when they think this way, they're not focused on what I'm teaching you. Those are force of average thoughts. You'll have them until you get your money right. And you have to get your money right before you can do anything else. You can have all the love in the world, but love won't buy you a bus ticket. It won't pay your mortgage. It won't pay for your kids' school. Once you get your money right, you can get everything else right. But the money comes first, and getting it right only works if you stay focused and committed. My life as an entrepreneur has been anything but a straight line up. I became a millionaire for the first time in 2005 and promptly lost it by 2007. Then I climbed my way back up to half-millionaire status by 2009 and lost it all in 2010.

Losing it all happens; it's a part of business. But when you get focused on doing the right tasks every day, you minimize your risk of sliding back down the ladder. You decrease the number of temptations that will distract you and come against you from the force of average. The weird thing is, you won't even see the distractions. Instead, you'll hone in on getting shit done. That's the real game changer. It doesn't matter if you own your business or work inside somebody else's business as what's called an intrapreneur. An intrapreneur is someone who gets shit done within a company. They're hired to focus on creativity and make initiatives profitable. I have several of them working for me. The point is, no matter your arrangement, what I'm teaching you about the grind will make you a success in your own right.

If you get to where you're finishing your job faster by following the code, start a side hustle. The bottom line is that business is the creator of money, and money is the fuel to fix everything. You can argue with me that this is not the case, but I'll argue right back. Money can fix damn near anything.

Staying focused is the way to accomplish whatever you want. You can use focus to bring value to the marketplace and improve processes, become a millionaire, billionaire, and trillionaire, complete your daily tasks, and win big in business.

The grind is not to be ignored. If you're not working for

yourself in your own business, that's okay. Just know that the grind is not to be ignored, no matter your work situation. The harder you work within any organization, whether you own it or not, the more you'll eventually be rewarded. Work harder than what your company pays you to do, and you'll be paid more than you're worth.

13

THE FOURTH G

G4: GROUP

The fourth and final G in the G Code is group. This is the group of people you surround yourself with most often.

I'm friends with a preacher whose favorite saying is, "Alignment takes precedence over assignment." What that means is that who you're aligned with—the folks that you hang around— is more important than whatever you were called to do on this planet.

You have an assigned divine favor on this planet. In other words, you were born to win. But most of us spend time with the wrong group of people. I know this is something you can relate to, because we've all been with the wrong crowd. We've all been around the do-nothing motherfuckers, the complainers, whiners, criers, and agents of average. Oftentimes, we came up with them. Folks who read books like this usually leave a lot of those kinds of people behind. They have to if they want to rise to new levels.

The group of people you hang out with is the most important predictor of your success on this planet. I've lived this truth.

I grew up in a small town with a few of my cousins who

never wanted to hang out with me. I didn't figure out why until later on in life when I realized that my family on my mother's side had banking issues, so those cousins had probably heard bad things about my family and me over the years.

Still, I felt like an outcast, so I started hanging out with another group of people. My cousins were the cool kids, and they didn't want to bother with me, so I hung out with other kids who just happened to be black. We lived in a small town, and this was not a normal thing. I was in second grade and hanging out with mostly black kids, not having a second thought about it. But unfortunately, hanging with these new kids made my struggles in school even harder. All the other close-minded kids were like, "I don't know what he's doing, man. He's hanging out with the blacks," or whatever. As a young kid, I didn't get it. I was just making friends with kids who wanted to be around me.

Then we moved to Allen and lived in a poor neighborhood. It wasn't the big city it is today. Poor neighborhoods are full of poor decisions. As a kid, I'd go over to my friends' houses and see them make poor decisions that I thought were totally normal. I'd see my parents make poor decisions too, and I thought *that* was totally normal. Then I got a job at a car wash, and we all know what kind of people work at car washes. There are definitely no Harvard-educated lawyers washing cars.

Before long, I found myself doing drugs and breaking laws.

In contrast, my kids are growing up in well-to-do neighborhoods. Their friends are from private school and church. They see people all around them—including their parents—making good decisions and winning in life because they're with the right group of people.

We don't get to choose our family of origin. But we can make choices to improve the circle of people we hang with. We can even pick new family members.

I believe there are two families: our family of origin and our family of choice. None of us get to choose our family of origin, which is comprised of our grandparents, aunts, uncles, parents, and siblings. These are the people who were born into our same bloodline. That's how we originated. That's what makes them our family.

But the more important group of people in your life is your family of choice. I've had to leave my family of origin and build a whole new family of choice—my wife and kids, friends, employees, and so on. Your family of choice consists of the people that you *choose* to be in your family.

Some of you have both types of family in one. Your family of origin *is* your family of choice. You've chosen to keep that relationship with your parents, brothers, sisters, etc. They become your family of choice. But as an adult, we can't let the people who are in our family of origin hold us back from greatness if they're toxic to us.

When I was writing my first book, I sent it out to a few family members, and after they read it, I reached out and asked, "What did you think?" I was all excited about it. But a few of my family members said, "If you publish this book, you're not going to be invited over for Christmas." I had to make a serious decision then. *Do I let two or three people influence me and change my mind, or do I go ahead and publish it?* I couldn't let my family of origin stop me from creating a family of choice, and that book has now gone on to inspire and help millions of people.

It was a tough choice, but I published that book—and I have not been invited over for Christmas since. However, I didn't get to choose these folks as my family. They chose to separate themselves from me. As hurtful as it was, I'm 100% okay with moving on from them because I have a family of choice today that I get to surround myself with, and this family supports me every day.

Too many people are stuck with a family of origin that's only trying to hold them back. Some people are even three, four, or five generations deep in the same godforsaken small town. They haven't wandered out because Grandma warned them about the monsters in New York City. They might have heard about the homeless people, beggars, and shooters in Los Angeles. They might have heard that Dallas, Texas, has terrible people, and they should stay clear.

When it comes to people who try to influence what you do, you have to see through the emotions you're feeling. You have to see through the peptide chemicals that are pumping through your brain that give you that love connection for the people who are your family of origin. You want to be aware of these chemicals and refuse to be influenced by them if you know your family of origin is toxic to you. No matter what, you have to do what's right for you to make the imprint and impact that you are called leave on this planet.

The same rule applies to your business. I used to hang around other sales guys. Since I outearned them, I felt like a big fish in a small pond. Once I leveled up, I also leveled up my friend relationships and my business peers. I'm typically the poorest guy in the room. Doing this gives me realistic yet big goals to chase after; it keeps me motivated and pumped because I'm around the right group of people.

I used to be friends with drug dealers, killers, and pimps. Now I'm friends with lawyers, politicians, doctors, accountants, millionaires, and CEOs. When you get around the right group of people, at the right time and at the right place, the right things happen. Conversely, when you get around the wrong group of people, all the wrong shit happens. As the guy who's been to prison, been divorced, and been bent over by business partners, I know what those wrong relationships are like.

That's why the group of people you're around is critical when you're following the G Code. If you're fat and unhealthy, for instance, the right group of people will tell your ass to get into shape. If you complain, whine, and are negative, the right group of people will tell you to straighten your fucking ass out. If you're losing and getting down on yourself, the right group of people will love you and get you back to where you need to be mentally.

When you have the right group of people in your life, all the right things start to happen.

If you're hanging around people who are the most elite version of themselves, you'd have to be a sociopath to want to be an average version of yourself. When I work out with my friends Heath Evans, Mike O'Hearn, and Jon Cheplak, I can see these guys are ripped. They're so ripped, statues after made after these motherfuckers. Todd Abrams is another person I aspire to be like physically. Being in the company of these guys makes me push myself to a level I might not otherwise.

I'm in great shape, but when I work out with them, I want to be in even greater shape. I see what's possible because I'm around the right group of people. If I hung around a bunch of people who were out of shape and could only do one pull-up, I would feel good about doing 10 pull-ups. Instead, because I'm with people in great shape, doing 20 pull-ups, I'm determined to do 25. Being around them makes me want to be the most elite version of myself.

If you're around the right group of people, they'll influence you to make the right decisions. It's almost impossible to hang out with elite people and be average. If you chill with a bunch of billionaires, you'll see how damn easy it is to do what they do and how realistic it is for you to become a millionaire. Surely, you can do 1% of what they're doing.

When you start hanging around people who are spiritually and mentally focused, they dial you in, too. That's why we have programs like Apex Coaching, where we're all dialed-in and focused. The right group of people in your life will help you live the right life that you were designed to live. So stop settling for mediocre friends. Stop settling for fucking average family members. Stop settling because somewhere along the line someone told you that you had to be loyal to the wrong people. Get rid of that thought process—it's not true.

Surround yourself with the elite, and you become the elite. That's how it works. Surround yourself with the average, and you stay fucking average.

Have you ever been to Los Angeles? The people in Beverly Hills, in their beautiful homes, are nowhere near the homeless people huddled together downtown. Just like the uber-famous and wealthy, the homeless have decided to stick together. Like attracts like. These two groups of people are vastly different from each other, but they're only a few miles away, on a different side of town.

Think of the conversations happening on skid row versus the conversations happening at the Beverly Wilshire Hotel bar. Alcohol is involved in both of these scenarios, on the street, and in the bar. Conversations are involved in both of these scenarios. The difference lies in the group of people having the conversations. This is more proof that when you get with the right people, the right stuff happens.

We make being successful and leveling up so much harder than it has to be.

Many of us have an addiction to codependence. We're attached to people who hold us back. They're the crabs in a bucket reaching out with their sharp claws to pull at our feet, calves, and thighs to get us back down into the bucket. But you're better than that. No matter what anybody's told you, you're better than that. The people who've told you that you weren't better merely wanted you to believe that you weren't— so they could keep you the same way you've always been. They want you to keep being an agent of the force of average—that's the person *they* are comfortable with.

Here's the great news. We live in a time where you can become friends with the elite in a matter of seconds, thanks to social media. You can choose your reality the same way you choose your newsfeed. When I log into my social media accounts, I don't see a bunch of political, religious, and angry posts because I've surrounded myself with the right group of people who talk about inspiring subjects. They talk about building; they talk about dominating; they talk about greatness. Reading these posts makes me happy.

Contrast that with the reality that most people get in their newsfeed, which is usually a bunch of bickering and drama. If you're living this, you have to change it. You have to get away from it. Negativity, anger, scarcity, fear, and lack make up the modern-day black plague that's killing human beings, so resolve to get these things out of your life. Your new life starts by getting around the right group of people. Follow the right leaders online. Show up at their events. Buy tickets to their seminars. Read their books. Listen to their free podcasts.

As soon as I had the extra money, I joined a country club. Since it was only a couple hundred dollars a month, it didn't take long to get a membership. I wanted to surround myself with people I wanted to be like, because the right group of people can make or break your life's path.

I want you to pause for a minute at the end of this chapter and make a list of everybody you've had contact with in the last six months. Record every person you've communicated with via phone call, text message, email, etc. in business and in your personal life. Next to each person, put a plus or minus sign. The plus sign obviously means you'll keep them in your life, and the minus sign means you'll leave them.

To assess whether each person will get a plus or minus, ask

yourself if they are taking energy from you or giving energy to you. When you get to the end of the list, all the people who are minuses need to go. All the people who give you energy and have earned that plus sign will stay. This is an important exercise because you want to add energy to your life. You don't want energy to be depleted from your life.

You're ready to remove the people from your life who have the minus signs. You don't have to be mean or rude. You just have to be busy all the time. That doesn't mean you need to make other actual plans. You'll simply tell the minuses you're busy whether you have plans or not. When they want to do something, give them this response every time, "I can't. I'm busy." Or, "That doesn't work. I have something else scheduled."

Eventually, those people will stop asking to hang with you. Sometimes they won't go away quietly, but most of the time, they'll simply stop asking. Breaking away is not as scary as you think. What's scary is surrounding yourself with a bunch of losers and settling for mediocrity in your life. What's scary is risking who you could be for who you are. What's scary is deciding to remain in the same place, as opposed to stretching yourself beyond your current reality and the only life you have. That's what's scary to me. It should be scary as hell to you, too.

14

LIVING THE G CODE

N ow that you know the four components that make up the focus points for the G Code, you need to learn and implement the G Code on a daily basis. In my office, we call this living the G Code. If you want to live a great life, be a great person, and have and achieve great things, you have to follow the G Code. Doing this isn't optional, and as I said, it won't change your life overnight.

The force of average would have you believe that following the G Code is an ineffective way of doing anything, but in the following pages, I'm going to share some stories about my personal journey and others' journeys that will prove to you how the G Code has truly affected our lives.

Because most people's attention spans are about 5 minutes long, when you talk to somebody about doing something for 90 to 100 days, a year, and even 10 years, everything you're saying falls on deaf ears. It falls on minds that can't comprehend the future because they can't even focus for 5 minutes.

I'm here to tell you that once you achieve focus, clear vision, and a process to make your vision a reality, you can no longer afford to make excuses. What you'll also learn in the process is that you aren't making excuses so much as you're making choices.

Like any bad decision, your poor choices will catch up to you. If you live on sweets and you don't eat protein and greens, you're going to develop diabetes and, most likely, cancer. Everyone knows that nowadays, so if you *choose* to go home and eat a bag of cookies, a Butterfinger, and a tub of ice cream regularly, you can't get mad at God. You can't get mad at medical technology. You can't get mad at cookies, ice cream, or sugar when you inevitably get seriously ill. You consciously made the decision to eat poorly, knowing that shit wasn't good for you.

The same thing applies when it comes to living the G Code. I'm going to walk you through the simplest, most undeniable way to be great in life every day. At this point, you have a decision to make. If you choose to live a life of mediocrity and not follow the G Code's daily process, that's fine, but recognize that it's a choice that you made. It's no different than deciding to survive off sweets and then suffering from diabetes.

The first thing I want to do is invite you to sign up for the app that will help you track your wins and decisions if you haven't done so already. It's 100% free, and I'm going to ask you to not share this link with people who haven't read this book. Go ahead and tell people to buy the book, and *then* they can get the app. But please don't give away the damn app with the cheat code. The G Code is not the cheat code.

Go to gcode.phonesites.com and enter your information. When you're asked for the invite code, enter: GREATNESS. Once you get the app set up, you'll realize the Daily G Code is not a traditional app—it's web-based software that acts like an app, but you don't have to download anything. You just add it to your home screen *like* an app.

Once you're on the site, you'll simply hit the arrow button on your Android or iPhone and save the URL as a bookmark on your home screen. You need to do this because you'll be using the website daily. When you're living the code daily, you need to track your process and progress quickly and easily.

The first area we talked about is G1: Gratitude. Every day, when you wake up, grab your phone and open up the Daily G Code app. You'll notice at the top of the Daily G Code, it will ask you for the five things you're grateful for. I don't care how many things you put in. You can enter 20, 30, 40, 50, or 100 entries if you want, although the code requires a minimum of five. Do this, and you get one point.

Listen, the force of average is going to try to piss you off in the morning. It's going to distract you. The force of average is going to make you mad when your day starts out with unexpected shit. That's why you need to do this first thing, before the day gets going, before you leave your bed. This is our new plan and the first step of the G Code. We're going to wake up and be grateful the very first thing in the morning.

We're going to train our brains to immediately wake up and search for something to be happy about and thankful for. We're going to search for something that's bringing us enjoyment, because plenty of stuff tries to bring us pain on a daily basis.

The second part of the G Code is G2: Genetics. The app is going to ask you, *Did you work out? Did you stick to your diet?* For some people, working out might mean running a marathon. For others, it might be a CrossFit session, boxing workout, Jiu-Jitsu round, weightlifting, or anything in between. Your job is to make sure that you work out seven days a week because maintaining and improving your genetics is crucial.

You also want to stick to some sort of diet. Again, you don't have to go full-blown keto or follow another fad diet religiously. But if you want to do that, and it's proven to work, that's awesome. The main goal is to pick a diet and stick to it. We don't want any roller coasters. If you want to be great, choose a predictable option and stick to it.

Let me tell you guys a little bit about genetics. Right now, as I'm working on this book, I'm wearing a neck brace because I broke my C7 neck bone. A cast covers my entire left arm because I broke two bones in a crash. I was driving a Razor Dune Buggy on a friend's deer lease and crashed, rolled, and flipped the damn thing twice.

I had to be CareFlighted out of the ranch to a military trauma hospital where I was worked on. It was a messed-up situation. What started off as one of the greatest weekends of my life—with a trip in a nice private jet to my friend's private airport on his land in the middle of his frickin' deer lease—turned into a life-changing event. The private jet was awesome, by the way, with a Come and Take It flag on the side of it; give them a whirl if you're looking for private transportation.

What was going to be an epic weekend changed so fast. I made a left a little too quickly on the dune buggy, and it caught a rut in the ground and flipped. I wasn't going fast. I wasn't showing off. The accident happened in the blink of an eye, and everything I was looking forward to was gone that fast, too. I was CareFlighted out of there, too, and released from the emergency room 15 hours later with a broken neck and arm.

While I was in the hospital, multiple doctors came in and talked to me. The neurologist, physician, orthopedic surgeon, and several other medical professionals all said a variation of the same thing: *It's a frickin' miracle, Mr. Stewman, that you're even alive, let alone that you're walking out of here. You were thrown over 12 feet from a utility vehicle without a helmet or seatbelt. Anybody else would have broken every bone in their body and been paralyzed. But because you're in phenomenal shape, you have enough muscle protection and bone density that you just barely fractured your neck and fractured some pieces of bone in your arm that should heal up in about six weeks. Then you'll be as good as new. You need to be very thankful that you're alive. You're a lucky man.*

I told them, "Thank you, but the truth is, I'm not lucky. I've been living the G Code and taking care of my genetics for 21 fucking years. Every day, despite not wanting to do it, I go work out."

Now, let me ask you this question: If you had the chance of a lifetime to fly on a private jet with me and go to a deer lease to do a little hunting and fishing and have a great time, and you got into that UTV with me, and I made that left turn and crashed, *could you have survived the crash?*

The guy who was in the vehicle with me also lives the G Code. He's in better shape than I am. He didn't have to go to the trauma emergency room. He went to the local clinic instead, got patched up, and walked right out of there. Could you do that? If anybody else had been in that vehicle with me, the chances of their survival would be slim to none.

Genetics are important. My friend, Dr. Matt Chalmers, talks about how he helps people who make up to $100 million when they exit from and sell their companies, but then these guys can't even get on an airplane because they're so out of shape. They can't see the world because they don't want to or can't walk around. My point is, you have to focus on your genetics. Get it out of the way every morning.

The third G is G3: Grind. When you fill out this part of the code, you'll need to ask yourself, *Where did I win at work? Where did I win in my mindset?*

Write down as many wins as you possibly can, that way, any time you're having a bad day, you can go back and look at your past days and see that you win every day. You're not a loser. You win every day. And your proof is in the Daily G Code app!

Next, you're onto G4: Group. Who are the people you spent time with today? Sometimes it's more than one person, but you need to make sure that you're giving to your group every day. That requires focusing on time with your kids, spouse, employees, and JV business partners (if you have them). Regardless of how your group is structured, write down whomever you spent your time with.

Focus on at least one person per day, and make it a different person every time. Do you go on date night once a week with your partner? Do you go on date night with your kids? Do you go on date night with your employees? I don't mean whether you take your employees out and try to impress them by buying them dinner and getting them drunk. I mean do you show them how much you value them? Do you buy them dinner and thank them for their help and for being a part of your team? The same goes for your friends. If you want to have good friends, you better be a great friend.

The last thing the app is going to ask you is, *What is the lesson that you learned today?* When you get to this point, take some time to reflect on the biggest lesson you learned that day. You can write as much as you want, but just make sure that you record your lesson.

To recap: Record what you're grateful for in the morning, then tackle your four Gs. Before you go to sleep every night, write down your wins, who you focused your time on, and the lesson you learned.

The next day, open the app and start the process again. At the end of the day, you get four points if you've done everything correctly. That means you can get 28 points a week.

Understand that, if, for example, you're only getting seven points a week because you're doing one-quarter of the work, that's not greatness. If you're only getting 14 points because you're only doing 50% of the work and you wonder why your life isn't together, there's your reason. Maybe you're making money and have a grateful mindset, but you can't attract a woman or get your health together. Take a look at where you're not giving your all. Are you not going to the gym? Are you not sticking to your genetic diet? Where else are you slacking?

Fix those issues and you'll quickly learn that when you look good, you'll attract good-looking people who will want to be with you and love you. It's the truth.

We try to fight this idea, but natural selection means that pretty chicks want pretty dudes and vice versa. This theory is proven when we see two overweight people together. Rarely do you see a couple with a super fit person and a super overweight person. I don't think I've ever seen that in my life, actually.

The long and short of your job as a follower of the G Code is that you will pull out this app to wake up with, and you will go to sleep with it. Within 30 days, using the app becomes a habit. And in six months, you'll look back and see that your scores are 500 and 600 points deep. That's the fun part—when you can reflect and say, "Shit! How much has changed in my life? Look at all my wins. Look at all these lessons I've learned. Look at everything I have to be grateful for!"

So, not only do you have the four areas to focus on every day, but you also have a free tracking mechanism that allows you to track those four things and how you focused on them each day. In 6 months, you'll become a hyper-focused, laser-targeted, goal-accomplishing machine, which is exactly what it takes to fight the force of average successfully. The bonus is that you'll do all this while attaining greatness the G Code way.

15

THE REALITY OF THE G CODE

Now that you know the four parts of the G Code that you must focus on to live a great life, now that you're aware of the daily process and the software that will give you the trackable, accountable, measurable success that you're looking for, you're at a point where you must make a decision.

You know what to do and how to do it. It's not complex. There's no excuse for you not to participate other than you're simply choosing good over great. I'm not here to force you to make that decision. I'm here to force you to live with the reality of the decision that you make.

But unlike most people, authors, books, and almost every other media or resource you're exposed to, I'm going to teach you here what to expect, how it will feel, and how to make it happen when it comes to living a great life and living according to the G Code.

There are three very specific phases of the G Code that you'll go through, but you can't rush them. It's just a matter of time and routine before each of these phases settles in with you.

The first phase you have to focus on is your score. You'll

notice inside the Daily G Code app that when you log in and complete your four things every day, you'll get four points.

As I explained, that's 28 points per week. Achieving greatness means you'll reach a true 28 points every single week. Anything less than that is not great; it's either good, okay, or horrible. If you did not nail every point you could, your ranking is not great.

Success leaves clues, and one of those clues is what gets tracked and measured; what's tracked and measured improves. When you start tracking and measuring on a four-point focus scale every single day, you chase the math. As a result, you put in the effort to get those 28 points every single week.

If you're a true 28, and not just hitting 28 points one week, while missing other weeks, you will achieve greatness. To do this, you need to hit 28 consistently every week that you're living the G Code—which will be every week of your life, right?

As you practice and progress, be aware that most books, gurus, and people in my position will try to sell you on believing that achieving greatness is based on divine enlightenment. They want you to think a spiritual high or meditative state will make you feel differently. I'm going to argue that point, because I know when you do this and follow along with the steps you need to take, you're going to be fucking great. When you achieve greatness, it isn't going to give you a buzz. If it does, awesome, but don't expect it. The G Code isn't going to create a newfound fucking high inside your head, but there are benefits. You know we're working on your genetics, so you should start to feel better.

If you're truly getting to 28 every week and putting in the work, you'll be stronger. When you're stronger, and when you feel better, you're more confident, and you're more grateful for who you are, which helps to create your grateful mindset. On top of that, when you look good, feel good, and are consciously competent, you tend to run into the right people. You get around the right group. These people can lead to jobs, income, JVs, partnerships, and everything else that bleeds over into your G3. But it all starts with the first phase of the code, and that's getting the numbers right. Your first goal is getting to 28 every week. That goal never changes.

You're not striving to hit it one week and feel like, "Fuck yeah," but then the next week, fall to a 17. That's force of average behavior. You were at 28. Why the fuck wouldn't you stay there? You don't want to peak and then regress. That's what the force of average would have you believe that you're supposed to do. It wants you to have a good month, then a bad month; lose a bunch of weight, then put it back on; find the dream girl, then cheat on her. It wants you to be a good dad, then piss off your kids; be an awesome mom, then not put in the effort you're supposed to. It wants you to be a shitty friend.

But when you're focused on that score and putting those points up every single day to get to your 28 every week, your perspective shifts from, "It's okay for me to be at 28 one week and 17 the next," to, "I am a 28."

I'd like for you to start posting that in your social media: "I am a 28." You are, if you're truly living by the G Code and doing what you're supposed to be doing. If you genuinely want to be great, you are a 28.

Here's the next thing to consider as you learn and live by the code: Never stop. When you move to the next phase, never stop. You don't want to get to phase two and then stop keeping score. These scores are cumulative. They go together.

Phase two of living the G Code is accountability.

If your paycheck is small, the people you surround yourself with are shitty, and your health is horrible, it's because you're not putting up the score. It's that simple.

The G Code gives you a four-point scoring system that

measures overall greatness in the four major areas of your life. It makes you accountable. If you're consistently a 10 or 20 and you don't look, feel, and have everything that you want, should have, and that you have earned, then you're not living by the G Code—you're not getting the right score.

You need the scoring tool because it holds you accountable. If your life isn't what you want, and you look at your score and see you're getting a 10 or a 20 every single week, the two are directly correlated. Your score and your life aren't coincidences. The score is there so that every day you'll create a routine of accountability and competitiveness. This happens because you're trying to hit a certain score every day, and you're getting in the routine of being that great person who's required to hit that score.

Do you see the compounding effect that occurs by taking a very simple four-point system that applies to four areas of your life and breaking it down daily and weekly with those simple numbers? When we do this, we have a scoring model for winning at life and an accountability partner to hold us to our word so that when we see we have a bad week and that it's directly related to the score, we know it's not just a coincidence. We know it's not that you had a bad week, so your score is low. It's the opposite. *Your score is low, so you had a bad week.* I want you to memorize that.

That's the thing about choosing to be great. That's the thing about aligning with the G Code. You can't bullshit yourself.

You can bullshit me. You can bullshit social media. You can bullshit your significant other, kids, employees, and people who fucking know you, but you cannot bullshit yourself. When you look down at your phone and see your numbers are low and you're knee-deep in bullshit without cowboy boots, you have an accountability model to change that.

Now here's what happens in the third phase—and this is the

beautiful part of this entire process—you gain focus. Suddenly, you're competitive because you've got a score to reach.

You're improving and accountable because now you have to face the fact that if your number is low and your performance is low, the two are directly correlated. This gives you routine focus. You're competing, and you're clear on what you're competing against. You're not competing against your competition. You're not competing against yourself. You're competing against the force of average and the score of four. That's it.

Most people live their life without a score to keep. That's why so many athletes peak in high school and college. Their game scores kept them competing for better scores—until they graduated and there was no longer a score to keep.

When these talented athletes get to work after high school and college, they don't think of money as a score. The competitive element goes away. There's no competition for them because they have a salary. They won't make more or earn a commission if they make a bigger score. This is why they're failing. They're keeping track of the wrong numbers.

In contrast, we have a scoring model for the rest of our lives, and that scoring model holds us accountable.

We know that if we want to be great, we've got to be 28.

When we live by the G Code, we're competing to be great every single day. We're competing against the force of average. We're putting numbers on the board each day of our lives, not on the board of the past high school football games we played.

Now we're putting numbers on the board every single day for the rest of our lives, and we're making sure that we want to be great. We're hitting 28 on a weekly basis.

After about 30 days, you'll move into the part of the accountability phase where you're competing and holding yourself accountable because of the Daily G Code app. After about 90 days, you'll get focused on putting those numbers on the board every single day, moving into the third phase. By this time, you've got a system, a service, and a smile on your face as big as the Grand Canyon. Now you're putting numbers up and winning every day.

You've even got proof that you're winning because you're using the Daily G Code app. You have proof that you're focused because you're tracking your focus on the Daily G Code app. You know that you're grateful because you're listing what you're grateful for every day inside the Daily G Code app.

The third phase of living the G Code, focus, makes you an unstoppable machine. When human beings are focused and in the zone, they cannot be stopped. When we get in the zone, we change maps. We explore intergalactic fucking space and time travel. We disrupt the banking systems. We overthrow economies. We influence the election of different leaders. When you enter the third phase of living the G Code and move into the focus phase of everything, you become an unstoppable machine that's on fire for greatness like you've never seen in your life.

That, my friend, is precisely why I wrote this book. It's precisely why I made this process. It's precisely why I want you to follow the steps as they are laid out—because they show you how to become great in life.

16

HOW TO WIN EVERY DAY

L iving by the G Code is the routine that you need every
single day in order to live what I call the perfect day.

Before you can live the perfect day, you have to define perfec-
tion. You have to define your focus.

Again, most people will say something along the lines of:

"I want to be a millionaire."

"I want to make a whole bunch of money."

"I want to be in good shape."

"I want to be healthy."

While those are good goals to have, they're too vague.

So you want to be rich. Well what's the definition of rich to
you? Is it having $100 million net worth with zero debt? Or, is it
having $100,000 net worth with zero debt? Everybody has a
different definition of success. They have a different definition of
being rich. Until you define what being rich means to you, you'll
never be able to focus, and you'll never have something to focus
on to make being rich a reality.

I'm going to share a routine that you can fall into every single day, like clockwork, so you'll go through the phases and be focused on the four areas that matter most.

But before you can focus on anything, you need predetermined goals. You can have all the power of focus in the world, but if you don't have anything to focus on, it doesn't do you any good. You can possess all the power needed to focus, but if you're focused on the wrong things, you'll continue getting results in your life that you won't like.

So, it's important that we establish what your goals are. If there are four areas that you must focus on every day, let's create four very specific goals that we're working toward in those areas.

The first G, G1, is a grateful mindset. Knowing this, ask yourself, *What is a goal that I could set, where a byproduct of working toward it would be having a grateful mindset?*

For me, it would be not being angry. My goal is to go consecutive days without being angry. My goal is never to explode again. If I want to never explode—because anger is a symptom of fear—I have to strive for the absence of fear. I have to believe in abundance. If I want to believe in abundance, I have to be grateful enough to believe that I can get what I need again. I know now that the only reason that I get angry is that I'm operating from a place of fear, so my goal is to be grateful enough to never be fearful.

G2 is genetics. When it comes to genetics, most people say, "I want to be in good shape," or "I want to be healthy." That's not enough, though. You've got to be more specific. For example: "I want to be 195 pounds with 13% or less body fat," or "I want to run five miles consecutively without stopping," are specific goals that allow you lay out the necessary steps to achieve them.

The third G, G3, represents the grind. My goal is to make $10 million a year. When you break that down, it's $23,000 a day. So my job, every single day, is to focus on $23,000 a day. That's pretty specific, and that's why I will get there.

The final G, G4, stands for group or family. This area represents the amount of love you want to have in your life. Do you want to have an exceptional marriage? Awesome. What's that like for me? I had to define what I wanted and what would work for both of us. My wife and I have sex four-plus times a week. We'll go out on a date night once a week. We take a vacation—just the two of us—at least twice a year. I provide things to keep my wife happy, such as an office manager who works from home and private school for the kids. If you want to have an exceptional marriage, you need to define what your goals will be in these specific areas.

Once you've taken the time to put these goals into very specific, focused definitions and you've broken down to the day, what you need to do to accomplish them, you can start the perfect-day routine.

To follow the perfect-day routine, the first thing in the morning that you need to do, before you get a drink of water, use the restroom, or do anything else, is pick up your phone, open up the G Code app, and type in the things you're grateful for. Remember, the more specific you can be, the better. I might write: *I'm grateful for Jackson because he is a good reflection of who I've become as a father. Jackson reminds me of how hard I've worked for him to get him to where he's at.*

Once you've done that, then you can drink your water, use the restroom, and do whatever else you need to do. But remember, before you go to work, you must work out. Right after you express your gratitude, you've got to work on your genetics.

My routine is that I wake up, write down five things I'm grateful for, have a protein shake, and then go to the gym. As I mentioned, I have a personal trainer. I have goals that I hit when I'm working out. I don't want to get to the gym and not put the effort in and then get fat again. I want to get there and fucking stay there to do the work to meet my goals. I don't hit the gym to say that I did it, like so many people do. That's force-of-average shit. I'm there, making an impact on my goal.

I already told you that science has proven working out in the morning is the best time for working on your physical health. If you want to be great, you have to be willing to do what most won't do. G Code peeps work out in the morning. We go to the gym. Remember, the app is going to ask you, *Did you work out?* So you need to get it done whether you work with a personal trainer or go to the gym and use the machines. Move your body and work out. That's all you have to do. You should have goals surrounding your physical fitness. When you see the question, *Did you work out?* Ask yourself, before you write down your answer, *Did I work out according to my goals?*

The next question is, *Did you stick to your diet?* We talked about the fact that you don't need to follow a specific diet. Just make sure you do your best not to eat a bunch of shit. That's the diet I live by, and that means I'm not going to eat Snickers, Kit-Kats, or Butterfingers. I'm not going to have an afternoon snack. Figure out a diet that's going to work to get you where you want to go genetically according to your goals. Then answer that question, and be honest.

It's time to go to work, G3. Work takes up most of our day. We'll talk about balance in a later chapter, but we do know that work takes most of our time—even as we strive for balance. Most of us work for 6, 10, 12, or 15 hours a day. While you're there, your job is to focus. As we talked about in Chapter 12: The Grind, being focused on a schedule that has every slot time-blocked makes all the difference in the world. You can turn what used to take 10 hours into two hours if you're focused, determined, and working according to a schedule.

We work for the day—no matter how long that takes. But at

the end of the day, we give back to the people that we love. After you've worked, whether you've had date night with your wife, gone to the park with your kids, had lunch with a coworker, or promoted an employee, you need to have taken action to invest in somebody else before you go to sleep at night.

Remember, you're going to open the G Code app again before you go to sleep. Open up the note you started earlier in the day where you wrote down the five things that you're grateful for. It's critical as you work the G Code that you do what you're assigned to do in each section of the code within 24 hours. You've got to do it that day. If not, you get cut off and don't get to finish that day.

Assuming you have completed what you were supposed to that day, you move on to, *Did you have any wins today?* This is when you ask yourself, *Did I do my $23,000 today? Did I hit a PR (personal record) in the gym today? Did something special happen at work?* Maybe you got a raise or promotion. *Did something special happen at home?* Take the time to think about, focus on, and concentrate on where you won. Type your wins in.

When you're living and working the G Code, you wake up first thing in the morning being grateful. You go to sleep in the evening with the last thing on your mind being where you won for the day. Talk about creating a good cycle of sleep! Talk about waking up happy and going to sleep a winner!

Move on to, *Who did you focus your time on today?* This question refers to giving back to our group. Did you do date night with your wife? If so, leave some feedback for yourself. It might be, *Did date night with the wife. We went to ___. We fought all damn night because I was an idiot and stressed out about work.* Be real with yourself. Did you take your kids to the park? What was that experience like? Did you go to lunch with one of your employees? What was that experience like? Did you get your friends together so you could have dinner? Did you do a double date with friends? Who was the person that you focused your time on? I don't mean, who sat next to you on the couch while you scrolled your phone. I mean, who did you focus your time on? Who did you pay attention to when they were talking? Who did you focus your time on listening to?

Move on to, *What is the lesson you learned today?* Take a minute to reflect on the day. You're going to be living the G Code for the rest of your life, so get used to taking the time to accurately record your experiences.

The mindset isn't that you're going to try this out for 90 days and then go back to the way you used to live. Don't forget, you're going to be living this code for the rest of your life. That means you're going to be stacking up a whole lifetime of wins and lessons, so take the time to fill out that box and note the lesson that you learned. If you learned multiple lessons, awesome, but at least write down the most important lesson of the day.

Now, once you input your lesson, close the app, hit save, and hit the hay.

Here's why this is the perfect-day routine. We're not worried about $10 million; we're worried about $23,000. We're not worried about being ripped and achieving 13% body fat immediately; we're worried about, *Did we go to the gym today? Did we stick to the diet that we set for ourselves?* The point is to set huge, audacious goals and then focus on the daily micro-commitments that allow us to live the G Code. When we approach achieving our goals this way, we can become that elite person we want to become.

Too many people set massive goals and don't have a routine to live by. I've just given you a simple four-step routine to live by and accountability software that pairs alongside it to help you make the most of the rest of your life—not just today or tomorrow, but from the time you ingested the content of this book onward. You now have the tools that have been used to succeed since the dawn of time. They've just been too fucking confusing until today. I've broken them down into four elemental areas of focus and given you monumentally simple software that will hold you accountable for life—and it's 100% free.

This is the legacy that I'm giving back to you. This is your opportunity to be the greatest, most elite version of yourself that you created in your mind when you completed the visualization exercise earlier in this book.

With the daily routine and the micro-committed points of focus that you must remain dedicated to daily to become the greatest version of yourself, you'll see an even greater version of yourself emerge than what you saw in your vision.

17

BALANCE IS A LIE

So far, this book has helped you outline what focus is, what the root of distraction is (AKA the force of average), why it's important to stay focused, what to get focused on, and how to set goals in conjunction with that focus.

In this chapter, we're discussing the biggest distraction the force of average throws at us. We're discussing what confuses people the most—balance.

We hear feedback all the time from the agents of average saying, "You need a work-life balance, man" as if those elements of our lives are the only two things that exist: work and life. The truth is, there's more than just work and family that makes up our lives. In this book alone, we've talked about the four major focuses that we have to concentrate on daily to live a life of greatness—a grateful mindset, the proper genetics, grinding it out at work, and having a group of people surrounding you that will help you become a better version of yourself.

Those are the four areas to focus on, but that doesn't mean that you have to balance them.

This whole work-life balance is bullshit. Why? Because it's

impossible. If we were going to balance something, and let's say it's at 100%, that means that 50% would have to go toward family, or "life" as this part of the balance is more commonly referred to. The remaining 50% would go toward work.

We'll assume that you work 10 hours a day and require a minimum of 6 hours of sleep. Now, most people sleep 8 to 10 hours. But minimum, you require 6 hours of sleep. That's 16 hours so far that you've used up. We're not counting traffic, gym time, or time focused on reading a book or personally developing yourself. We're not counting traveling or anything else. Sixteen hours out of 24 hours a day is already spoken for. That means you have 8 hours left over if you *only* work 10 hours a day. Some of us work a lot more than that! Remember, this doesn't count commute time. In places like Houston, New York City, and Los Angeles, commuters can take up to 3 hours to get to work—one way. Boil it all down, and the remaining 8 hours is where you're supposed to squeeze in the rest of your life and spend quality time with your family.

It's impossible to achieve a work-life balance. But that's what the force of average uses to distract everybody on this planet. Think about this: it uses a concept that doesn't exist. This harmonious existence between work and life doesn't exist. Isn't it trippy when you think about it this way—that we base success in our lives on hitting an equation that's imaginary? That's called setting yourself up to fail.

That said, there is a balance we *do* need in our lives. Balance plays a big part in who I am internally and how I think. My astrological sign is Libra, which is a scale. I'm a big believer that for every action, there's an equal and opposite reaction, and this applies to the balance we should strive for, because balance creates momentum. The real balance that we need to create in life is finding gratitude while striving for more.

No other balance is going to work.

Let me break it down.

When we try to balance work and life, we assume we're trying to balance life on the few hours that aren't eaten up by work. We believe that life is going to bring our time at work down. Of course we feel this way! There's not much left over to dedicate to life after work.

We all think we have to sacrifice going to work, changing the world, and making money so we can go home and hang out with the five people that we decided to bring into our world. That's why work-life balance has a negative connotation.

But striving to hit the balance between gratitude and wanting more doesn't take away from anything. It only stacks the momentum and the reward for growth. If you're like most people, chasing a balance that leaves you stagnant leads you to average; this is why you're struggling with hitting that work-life balance. And remember, this is a nonexistent balance. You're never going to hit it, and not hitting it over and over again is depressing.

If I would've never told you about seeking the gratitude balance, you would have been seeking it by default because you're living by the G Code. Now, I'm going to open your eyes to whole accountability, whole lifestyle, and a whole adaptation of what living a life of greatness really means. It's not complicated.

Being grateful for where we are while still searching and pushing for what's next is a life changer and game changer for you. Most people become extremely grateful for where they are and don't balance out their life and work. That's when they decide to settle. *Well, I have a good enough job. I'm grateful for that. I have a good enough spouse and good enough kids. I'm grateful for that. I have good enough health. I'm grateful for that. I have a good enough attitude. I'm grateful for that.*

When we're settling, we get super grateful and think that it's humble to be poor. It's humble to be average. It's noble to be poor. It's noble to be average. But it's not.

The polar opposite of uber-gratitude is what you find in the guys and girls who are always searching for what's next. They've got everything right in front of them, and they're not even paying attention to it. They're always anxious. They move around a lot, and they're awfully shifty. They're judgmental. They're unappreciative. They're focused 100% on what's next, so they never take a moment of their lives to enjoy what's in the now. They're never present and don't want to be. Maybe they wouldn't even know how to be.

This is what happens when you switch your focus to achieving a gratitude balance.

When you become grateful for every single thing you have right now in your life, but you're still focused on getting everything you've ever wanted, you're striking the true balance that creates momentum. It's not the force of average telling you to work in life, but the reality of greatness that tells you what's between what you have and what you want. It keeps you hungry and appreciative that you can eat at the same time.

We should never settle.

Remember, there are four levels to the workforce. We start off as sales professionals or people who work for somebody else, then we graduate to becoming entrepreneurs. Once we become entrepreneurs or self-employed, we grow on to become executives/CEOs. Then we sell our companies and become investors.

So many people get to a stopping point along the road of reaching these mile markers. Others follow the path to achieving more and have people ask them, "When's enough, enough?"

Who says I have to stop? Who says *you* have to? If you love what you do, and you enjoy doing it, the force of average will try to distract you away from it in every way possible. People will tell you that you're not balanced in your work. The force of average will have you believe that you haven't done enough and that you should sell your company, so you sell it, but now what? You have money, but nothing to drive you. Tell me: *Why would you stop?*

Remember my doctor friend who works with super-wealthy individuals who sell their companies after years of hard living or not giving a shit? When they sell, they want to enter a new phase of life and enjoy leisure time, but they can't even take pleasure in their money because they aren't healthy enough. Shortly after selling, many of them pass away because they don't have anything fueling them for what's next in their lives.

Don't let that be your problem, too. You don't need to stop if you don't want to.

The balance that we're looking for is the balance between being grateful for what we have while in pursuit of what's next. I never want to be so thankful for what I have that I'm no longer interested in growth. And I never want to be so focused on what's next that I don't take the time to appreciate where I am.

Don't forget, work and life are just two small chunks of our existence we have to balance out. We have to balance out our minds. We have to balance out our families. We have to balance out our genetics. You're striking the balance between eating food that you love and eating just enough of it so you don't get fat. You're striking the balance between being a good father and having to discipline with pain sometimes when your kids need to be spanked. There's always a balance that we're striving for. Work and life are just two very small things on a larger scale. But when you're focused on the G Code, your wins, and the four key areas of your life where you need to succeed, the smaller details handle themselves.

Grateful mindset, genetics, grinding it out at work, the group of people around you, and your focus on winning in those areas every day—that's what's going to create your work-life balance.

Your life feels more balanced because you're focused on date night with your spouse. You're focused on date night with your kids. You're focused on showing up for your friends. You take care of the group of people you're in. You're showing up for your grind, making your money, breaking records. Work and life don't need to be balanced at a zero. Life is not a net-zero operation. Balance your thought process between being grateful for what you have while being in pursuit of what's next. That's how you create real momentum.

As human beings, we were created to continuously grow. There's no stopping point for us until we no longer exist. Don't fall into the trap of believing you have to stop.

At this point in the book, you have a focus, purpose, and the software to hold you accountable. You have inside information on the balance that you need to strike so you can live your greatest life possible.

This is the G Code.

18

REPRESENT

One of my core values is that I represent what winning looks like at all times.

As you finish up this book, I want you to understand what being great is—what winning is. Remember earlier, when I had you focus on the most elite version of yourself? You focused on what that person would look like, what that person would feel like, and what that person's life would be like. Then I had you step in and become that person.

You may need to do that exercise twice a year, because as you become more elite, you'll realize that you can always become more elite.

That elite version of yourself is what it looks like when you win in every area of your life. That's the whole purpose of the exercise.

Now that you understand the G Code, it's your job to start acting as if you're that person every single day. When you do this, you'll become that person. I'm not saying to fake it till you make it. I'm saying that you should do what you would expect that elite version of yourself to do right now.

Living like that person starts with representing what winning looks like at all times. If you're going to live a life of greatness and fight the force of average, you have to be great at all times.

This reminds me of a story. My oldest son gets in trouble now and then, like any kid. One day, I told him, "You're such a good boy, and you make good decisions when you want to." He looked up at me as I went on. "Here's what I need you to do. When your mom and your brothers are around, I need you to make good decisions and be a good leader, okay?"

A few days later, a couple of my friends, my son, and I were all hanging out. My kid was acting like a damn fool, so I pulled him over to the side and said, "What's wrong with you? You're making all of these bad decisions. What about what we talked about? Did you forget what I said already?"

He looked up at me with his big blue eyes and said, "Well, Dad, you told me that as long as my brothers or Mom was around, I needed to make good decisions. But they're not around," he argued with a mischievous look in his eye, "so I get a chance to make bad decisions." I didn't know whether to be impressed by his thought process or scold him more. "I didn't know, Dad," he said quietly, "I thought it was going to be okay."

When he was talking, I realized something. How he described his way of thinking is how most of us think. We think that if we make decisions to have a good time, over a long period of time, then we *deserve* to make bad decisions. But a life of greatness is a life created from *compound* good decisions and representing what winning looks like *at all times*—even when Mom isn't in the room.

I see people in the airport when I travel, looking like they just rolled out of bed. But they're getting ready to hop on an airplane!

They don't comb their hair. They're sporting some wicked butt sweat. They smell, and yet they're out in public traveling the world in front of thousands of people! In contrast, I represent what winning looks like at all times. Whether you see me in the gym or in the office, it doesn't matter. I'm a 10 at all times. I shower and don't sport butt sweat. And even in a T-shirt and jeans, my clothes are clean. My shoes are clean. I wouldn't feel good walking around like a slob; it's bad for my mental health. I also know that this is what it takes to represent what winning looks like. It takes effort. But I want people to see me and say, "You look like you're winning, dude! What's your secret?" Winning looks like I give a shit about myself.

Then I let them in on the secret and tell them, "It's the G Code."

I want you to do the same thing. I want you to represent what winning looks like every single day in every area of your life. I want people to ask you what you're doing to seem so put together. Then you get to share the good news of the G Code, too.

The G Code has changed the lives of the people who live it. We deserve to represent the greatest versions of ourselves. When people see us, we should be saints in their eyes. We should be the elite. We should be heroes. We should be the people they look up to because we don't get caught slipping—we don't slip. We represent greatness at all times. We don't take a day off from being great! We don't wait until we have to behave and clean up to be great. We make being great an unbreakable habit.

We're great no matter what.

Bad decisions never yield good results anyway. Why take a day off to make a bad decision? Why do we celebrate those bad decisions? I see you and your girls going out drinking. I see you getting wasted in Mexico.

In Mexico, I once saw a guy who was smashed drunk get into a cab. In the newspaper a couple of days later, I read that he didn't make it home. One bad decision was all it took.

When I was out on that Razor and crashed, one bad decision was all it took. That was a lesson learned for me, and it sunk in deep. I could have lost everything in a split second. Why would I ever take my eyes off what I should have been focused on? Why would I ever want to take the chance of losing what I've worked so hard to build to a bad decision? Why would I ever want to go back to where I started? Why wouldn't I force myself to continue representing what winning looks like in every area of my life so that people will see me and want to model what I have?

Not because I, Ryan Stewman, want to be important, but because I, Ryan Stewman, represent the G Code. And that's much bigger, much greater, and much, much more important than I will ever be. It's your job, too—representing the G Code and showing the world your greatness.

If you live a life of greatness, then you're a winner. When we think about the greatest people of all time, we think about those standout performers: Mohammed Ali, Babe Ruth, Warren Buffett, etc. When you hear someone reference, "The greatest of all time" in any area of life, the first thought that comes to mind is a winner.

To be a winner, you have to do what you do better than anybody else. So if you're going to represent winning at all times, you need to do it better than anybody else. You don't get to be in front of the video camera and pretend like you give a shit about people and then talk to your employees about your customers like you couldn't care less about them.

You don't get to live that double standard. You don't get to be a hypocrite. You represent one side of the fence every day: the winning side. You're winning at home with your family. Not just publicly, but privately—you're working on your relationships to grow closer to people. You're winning in the gym by setting growth and personal records. You're winning with your genetics with the number of calories you're taking in and the amount of weight you're cutting. You're winning with the genetic, self-imposed diseases that are now reversing because you're eating right and exercising.

You're winning at work because you're focused, not scatter-brained. You're making the most of the time while you're there. You're an efficient machine because you understand your areas of focus in the G Code and scheduling your day out. Your friends and family don't have their hands out because you're making more money; they have their hearts out because they finally get to love the purest version of you.

Here's the greatest thing: Being a winner magnifies who you are. You'll see when you start to win that you get more love, you get more money, and you attain better health. You win across the board and become more of who you really are. Most of us, deep down, are really good people! The bad things that we've done over time happened because we weren't winning. They happened because we were losing money, love, and respect.

But when you consistently win, you have nothing to lose—because *you don't lose.* Instead, you're given opportunities every day to win across the board. Your confidence is through the roof, and people want to be just like you because people are attracted to winners. It's as great as it sounds, and I'm living proof of this every day.

Making the decision to live by the G Code doesn't mean that you get to take the weekends off. It doesn't mean that, when nobody's looking, you get to live by a different code.

This is a lifelong decision. This isn't a 90-day challenge.

I have outlined for you the four things that you must focus on for the rest of your life. I have created a scoring and account-ability system that you need to live by to reach your greatness. As I've often said, the whole planet is run on numbers; the G Code is no different. The G Code is the formula to greatness.

A fad's a fad, and before we know it, there'll likely be

millions of people living by the G Code. But in three or four years ... and God, I hope I'm wrong ... there'll only be thousands left who are living and thriving by it.

I'm over 900 days into the G Code. That means I've created daily logs for 900 days. If you were to scroll back through my social media, read my old books, look at my old blog posts, and watch my old videos, you'd see that I not only look completely different, I *am* completely different.

Until I found the G Code, I was lost. Until the G Code rescued me and gave me something to focus on, I didn't know what was next in life. But if you look back, you can literally see the pivot point in my life online, where the G Code became a part of my life. I was doing the G Code even before I knew what it was called. When the G Code became a part of my life, I became the person you know today.

I took a step into becoming the most elite version of myself and kept stepping until I became that man. Today, I am who I saw myself as in 2017 when I first did that exercise. The next step for me is a lot of even harder work, especially since I'm now 40 years old.

Greatness never ends. Growth is always expected.

Now that you live by the G Code and have made the decision that this is your way of life, there's no going back.

You are now obligated to meet the core value of representing what winning looks like at all times, no matter what. At work, at home, in the gym, at the airport, on vacation. Winners don't take days off from being winners. Greatness doesn't take a day off to be good.

You are destined for greatness. You are a winner. Represent.

AFTERWORD

Let's recap what I've shared with you in this book.

We've learned what it means to be elite. We've learned the importance of accountability. We've learned about the force of average and how it conspires to keep us average in all areas of our lives. We know how it conspires to keep us from achieving greatness. We've discovered that the ultimate combatant to the force of average is focus, and the ultimate companion to focus is accountability. We know that when we pair goals with specificity and focused action tracked by accountability, we become unstoppable.

Now, you get to truly live the life of focus, and you don't have to focus on 50 areas. You only have to focus on four. You don't have to focus on huge goals. You only have to focus on winning daily micro-commitments.

The biggest lesson that you can learn from this book is that when it comes to distractions, you're weak. You don't need an ADD/ADHD drug. You don't have attention deficit disorder. You're just losing the war against the force of average.

If you're having good months followed by bad, whether

that's in your genetics, the workforce, or at home, whatever it is, it doesn't matter—you're falling victim to the force of average. Now you know how to fight it, and you know that the most powerful weapon against it is focus.

Before this book, you never knew exactly what to focus on. Without a trackable and measurable process, you were just going through life, hoping you were focused on the right thing. If you were like most people, you spent your entire life telling yourself that you couldn't focus.

All that changes now. Now you get to continue to become the most powerful version of yourself. You get to tap into your own empowerment. You can do this because you have the knowledge of how to create a habit and routine, making you absolutely unstoppable.

When you're absolutely unstoppable, you have power. When you have power, you have control. Power is what we're all looking for. Energy is power. Knowledge is power. Applied knowledge and action is power. Control is power.

But if power is not focused, it becomes useless. Many of us were powerful individuals before we read this book, and now that we know where to focus our power, we're even more powerful. Many of us were energetic, active, healthy, and winning across the board; we were just uncertain of where to focus. The G Code is your first step toward focused power.

You've been set free, educated, awakened, and now you've been given a process. The G Code is not a religion, indoctrination, or condemnation. Living the G Code is a lifestyle decision. Those who choose to live it their entire lives will create power beyond belief. They will die legends.

You, my friend, are a very powerful individual. You've taken the time to get to the end of this book. "One in four Americans didn't read a single book in the last year."[4] So the fact that you're reading this book means something. Thank you for taking the time to invest in yourself and learn about the G Code.

I'm glad to share this journey with you. I'm glad to share these experiences, this knowledge, process, and plan for life. My goal is that it touches your life 10 million times harder than it's touched mine.

All it takes is your daily dedication to the G Code—following the process, holding yourself accountable with the 30-day challenge, and living your best life as a winner all day, every day. You can become a distraction-free, powerful machine—because now you know what you need to do.

Welcome to greatness.

You are the G Code.

REFERENCES

1. Ron Marshall, "How Many Ads Do You See in One Day?" Red Crow Marketing, September 10, 2015, https://www.redcrowmarketing.com/2015/09/10/many-ads-see-one-day/.

2. Nick Skillicorn, "Are you one of 2.5% of people who can multitask?" Idea to Value, June 24, 2016, https://www.ideatovalue.com/curi/nickskillicorn/2016/06/one-2-5-people-can-multitask/.

3. Jamie Ducharme, "This Is the Best Time of Day to Work Out, According to Science," Time, February 27, 2019, https://time.com/5533388/best-time-to-exercise/.

4. Kerri Jarema, "How Many Books Did The Average American Read In The Last Year? This New Study May Surprise You," Bustle, April 19, 2018, https://www.bustle.com/p/how-many-books-did-the-average-american-read-in-the-last-year-this-new-study-may-surprise-you-8837851.

ABOUT THE AUTHOR

Ryan Stewman has had anything but an easy life, from being adopted at age 7, to dropping out of school at 15, to being incarcerated at 20. Despite these and many more tragic setbacks, Ryan has been able to adapt and fluidly move around pretty much every obstacle that's ever been thrown his way.

Ryan's first job was in sales at age 13. He sold car wash upsells to patrons in Plano, Texas. He continued to sell car washes until he was 23 years old. This gave him tens of thousands of opportunities to get better at sales. By the time Ryan was 24, he was the top producer at a mortgage company in Frisco, Texas. At age 25, Ryan became a millionaire for the first time.

Although life was going great, Ryan was mistaken for a drug dealer, and the Allen, Texas, police department raided his home. They found no drugs (Ryan would pass a drug test the very next day) but they found a gun. That gun was left behind by Ryan's adopted dad and the dad refused to claim it. Despite all of this, Ryan beat the case and got the case dismissed. He sought to sue the City of Allen and they turned his case over to the ATF.

Ultimately, Ryan lost everything, including his wife and his freedom. On June 15, 2007, Ryan walked into FCI Seagoville a married millionaire. Less than 90 days later, he'd be flat broke and divorced. His wife took it all and went with another man. Talk about salt in the wound.

Ryan was released on July 11, 2008. After a few months, he got a job at a mortgage brokerage. He went on to become the top producer, single-handedly producing 9 figures in mortgages in less than 2 years. No team. No staff. Just hustle muscle. Ryan became one of the top loan officers in the country, despite 2009 being the worst year on record to be in mortgages.

In 2010 President Obama signed a law called "Dodd Frank" which changed mortgage licenses from state-controlled to federally-controlled. The feds denied Ryan's license and he lost the ability to do the only real job he had ever worked. Talk about another devastating blow.

Despite these setbacks and more, Ryan kept on focusing on his dreams, goals, and aspirations. No matter how many times life punched him square in the face, he knuckled up and fought back. Ryan attributes his focus and unwavering pursuit of his dreams to the GCode. Without this simple, accountable, daily process, he says he'd never be where he is now.

He's coached over 17,000 clients. He's got social media exposure of over 2 million followers. He's the CEO of 9 different multi-million dollar per year companies, such as Phonesites.com, Break Free Academy, and Wolfeman Assets. Ryan is regularly featured in *Forbes*, *Entrepreneur*, *Huffington Post* and many other massive publications. He's a best-selling author and a best-seller all around!

Ryan lives in Dallas, Texas, with his wife Amy and their three sons Jax, Asher, and Colton, otherwise known as Jax Dizzle, Ursher, and The Senator.

RESOURCES

JOIN THE #0to100 CHALLENGE TODAY at:
GCode.Phonesites.com

A daily writing app to help you document and improve your life. Track your score, streaks, and daily entries.
DailyGCode.com

Tune in to Ryan Stewman's Business Podcast:
Rewire Podcast